Passive Income Streams:

How to Create and Profit from Passive Income Even If You're Cash-Strapped and a Little Bit Lazy (But Motivated)!

Kristi Patrice Carter, J.D.

Copyright © 2016 Kristi Patrice Carter, J.D.

All rights reserved. No part of this book may be reproduced or transmitted in any form or by any means, electronic or mechanical, including photocopying, recording, or by any information storage and retrieval system, without written permission of the publisher, except in the case of brief quotations embodied in articles or reviews.

Disclaimer

This book is designed to provide factual information in regard to the subject matter covered. However, it is based on personal experience, interviews with other passive-income seekers, and research conducted by the author and her freelance staff. Although much effort was made to ensure that all information in the book is factual and accurate, this book is sold with the understanding that the author assumes no responsibility for oversights, discrepancies, or inaccuracies. This book is not intended to replace financial, investment, legal, accounting, or other professional services. If these services are required, the reader should seek out a competent professional. Readers are reminded to use their own good judgment before applying any ideas presented in this book.

ISBN: 978-1536919028

For further information, contact:

Thang Publishing Company
332 South Michigan Avenue, Suite 1032, #T610
Chicago, IL 60604-4434

Table of Contents

Acknowledgments 1

Introduction 3

1. Let's Get Started 11

2. Easy-Peasy Methods 16

3. Online Shopping Portals 28

4. Getting Paid to View Ads by Online Reward Companies 31

5. Selling Your Creative Talents 40

6. Writing eBooks and Print-on-Demand Books 42

7. Creating Udemy Online Courses 47

8. Blogging for Cash 49

9. Outsourcing - Utilizing the Skills of Expert Freelancers 54

10. Affiliate and Network Marketing 57

11. Email Marketing 60

12. Designing and Selling T-Shirts 65

13. Selling Your Photos 67

14. Starting Your Own YouTube Channel 70

15. Crowdfunding 72

16. Peer-to-Peer Lending 73

17. High-Interest Banking 101: Alternatives to Banks 77

18. Credit Card Rewards 82

19. Selling Web Design Templates 87

20. Music Licensing 90

21. Creating an App 94

22. Renting Properties 97

23. Investing Online 103

Conclusion 107

BONUS 109

About the Author 115

Acknowledgments

This book is dedicated to:

My loving husband and best friend, Delanza Shun-tay Carter, for encouraging me to write this book, for being supportive when I wanted to give up, and for his innate ability to occupy the kids with various activities so I could complete this book.

My daughter, Kristin Carter, and my sons, Shaun Carter and Daniel Carter, for listening to me read my drafts, offering great advice, eating breakfast for dinner, and encouraging me to "get that book done" so we could do something fun!

My mom, Christina Tarr, who has always offered unwavering love and support, helped out in every way possible to make my writing dreams a reality, and encouraged my writing efforts (from my very first story about a sick little girl named Nan who stayed home from school to the crafting of this book many years later).

My father, Lavon Tarr, for loving me, being a great dad, and not complaining when Mom came over.

My grandmother, Fannie Lee Richardson, for her incredible strength, consistent faith, and positive attitude while going through her own medical challenge and emerging victorious.

My mother-in-law, Michelle Carter, for unselfishly making delicious meals and treats for the family; and my father-in-law, Barney Lee Carter, for picking up the kiddos; and to both of them for always willingly helping out in a pinch to accommodate my writing time.

My best friend, Angela-Whitaker Payton (Moinks); my adopted mom, Darlene Norem-Smith (Mama D); my sister, Dana B. Robinson; Aunt Barbara Rhodes; Aunt Patricia J. Ray (Patty Cake); cousins Alison Turner-Graham and Chanda Taylor-Conrad; adopted grandmom Gladys Crump; and all my other amazing family members and friends (not mentioned here) who encouraged me to write my book and to never give up on my dream of helping others!

My researchers, motivators, idea generators, and best writing buddies, Geradina Tomacruz and Christy Mossburg; my editors, Denise Ann Barker and Amy Shelby; my proofreader, Meredith Dunn; and my graphic designer, Alex, for designing my dynamic eBook cover. Without your assistance, this book would not have been possible.

Finally and most important, I would like to give a heartfelt thanks to all the passive-income seekers who are reading this book. I understand that obtaining passive income isn't easy and takes effort, commitment, and perseverance. However, if you're willing to put in the work, you will surely reap the benefits. I applaud you for taking the first step to make your passive-income dreams a reality. You can do this!

Introduction

Let me tell you a little secret.

I love money. I love making it. I love the freedom it gives me. I love the way it feels when I have some in my pocket and in my bank account. I love the things that money can buy for me, my friends, and my family.

But I hate working a 9-to-5 job to make it.

Now I have the highest respect for those who work a traditional job. I admire people who grind day in and night to support themselves and their families by working for someone else. They've got tenacity, spunk, perseverance, and deserve all the accolades that we can give them.

But that type of career is not for me.

Something about clocking in and clocking out to make money just turns me off. Something about having to work a dead-end job that sucks the life out of me gives me the employee heebie-jeebies and worker procrastinitis. (Both conditions are very real and hurt like hell. Neither feels good at all.) I shudder to think about them.

So the way I avoid these negative feelings is not to work. OK, I work but not a traditional job. Instead I work on creating my dreams and fulfilling my goals. I work on making passive income streams—little streams of income that bring me money (day in and day out) regardless of whether or not I work that day.

I'm an entrepreneur and a rule-breaker at heart. **My passive income streams allow me to break traditional work expectations and still earn a living.**

These passive income streams allow me (and you too, if you dare) to game the system by working smarter, not harder.

Whether your streams come from writing books or blogs, running a profitable online store, lending money to people who need it in exchange for interest, or something else, these passive-income streams work *for* you. They make your life more pleasurable and improve your bottom line.

This way you can be the boss. You can choose the projects you work on. You can choose the clients you work for and fire the ones who get on your nerves. You can do the things you enjoy and never look back, all the while knowing that your financial needs are being met (and then some).

You can do the things you want to do without worrying about paying the bills. You can have fun and get paid too.

Take me for instance—yesterday I wrote like a maniac for eight hours straight, and, the day before that, I did nothing but watch the cold hard cash roll into my bank account from my passive-income endeavors as I lounged on the beach with my family.

I no longer feel like a slave to my job. **I no longer work a certain number of hours every day to make a set amount of money every week.** I can work hard when I want to or not work if I choose to, and I still make money. The passive-income life feels damn good.

So I've finally admitted what I've known all along deep down but was too scared to say aloud. The truth is that I am living a life of freedom and no longer care if other people think I'm lazy because I don't work every single day to make money.

And you know what? Freedom feels incredible. Thanks, passive income! Thank you very much.

This isn't to say that I got to this point by doing nothing every day. No, that's not what I'm saying at all. Initially I had to work, work, work, work, work. I had to create multiple passive income streams. Some days I worked for hours and other days I didn't. I created these streams at my own pace, in my own time.

When the mood hit me, I created and nourished my passive income streams. I found and watered the seeds, making sure they got sunlight. I plucked the weeds of frustration and waited. With patience and perseverance, most of the seeds are budding and bearing fruit. Now I am growing tasty prosperous fruit that feeds me every day, whether I'm working at home or hanging with family at home.

Sound like fun? You bet it does. There's no secret to my success. You can do this too! I don't have a secret playbook, so I'm happy to teach you what I know.

But you need a dream. You need a dream for freedom, the ability to put in a teeny bit of work, and a passive-income action plan. If you've got the dream, I've got the plan, and together we can make this money thing happen!

Consider me your mentor. I will teach you various passive income streams and show you how to monetize each one so that you soon have your own flourishing passive-income garden. Use all of these ideas or some of them. For variety I'll give you some that are easy-peasy, others that are a little harder, and a few extremely complicated ones.

Most will require no start-up funds, but some will require a little start-up capital. Some will be riskier than others. Some will yield an immediate return on your investment, and others will take more time to turn a profit. However, all of them will require a bit of time and effort to get started but will be worth it if you work the plan.

Like me, you can build these income streams at your preferred pace. You can change your life—one passive income stream at a time. With the additional income, you can prepare for an emergency or free yourself from the stress and worry caused by not having enough money to do the things you want to do. You can achieve happiness, freedom, and inner peace. Financial freedom will be yours!

Passive versus Active Income

So does passive income sound like something that interests you? I hope so.

To ensure that we're on the same page, let's define what passive income is and what it isn't.

The term *passive income* is broad and quite general. To be more specific, passive income is revenue earned when you aren't actively working for the earnings you obtain from an initial work project. But you don't have to be materially involved in this project to keep funds flowing. Passive income doesn't require your weekday involvement of eight hours a day or more, like a typical day job; that is *active income*. Active income requires you to work consistently in order to get paid. If you don't work, you don't get paid. It's that simple.

Book royalties are an example of passive income; you work initially, when writing the book, but don't have to put in a certain amount of hours daily in order to receive royalty payments. Other examples of passive income include real estate rental income, stock dividends, bank interest, peer-to-peer interest payments, and much more. Surprisingly, some people even make passive income watching ads on their phones or computers or selling their personal data to data-mining companies.

The main difference between active and passive income is that passive income enables you to be paid even when you're not doing consistent daily work. With active income, however, you must work consistently to get paid.

Now some of you might argue that passive income is risky and isn't as secure or stable as active income. But, honestly, is any job secure these days? With all the downsizing and mergers so prevalent over the last couple decades, it doesn't look like it. Big corporations and the like are giving fewer and fewer benefits, like yearly raises and matching 401ks. Is any business immune to unforeseen market changes that could cause it to go out of business? While I agree that passive income may be seen as a little riskier than active income, there are ways to eliminate these risks by having multiple streams of passive income and not relying on just one or two.

Call me a risk-taker but I'd take calculated risks—with an opportunity for bigger payouts and more freedom—rather than live a mundane soul-crushing life where I'm obligated to work hard every day to earn a steady paycheck. The very thought drains me, whereas passive income refreshes me.

Hang on a freaking minute ...

There's got to be a catch ... right? If it were so easy, wouldn't everybody be earning passive income? I wish they were, but that's not the case, even though most people want financial freedom. They just don't understand that working for someone else day in and day out typically only makes their bosses richer. They see passive income as something for billionaires and don't realize that everyday individuals with smaller nest eggs are building solid financial success with passive income every day.

Ask around and most of your friends will tell you that passive income costs too much to start. Or they'll state that it is too much work, too complicated, or simply too risky. They'll argue that the best way to build financial freedom is to work hard at a good steady job, save 10% or more of your income, retire early, and then enjoy all the money you've accumulated (even though, by then, you'll be too old to enjoy it).

My mind-set, and the one I hope you'll adopt, is a bit different though. I believe it's our duty to work hard when we feel like it, create passive income streams that will produce even more income later, and enjoy the fruits of our labor now—not when we retire. Heck, with enough passive income streams, we can hopefully retire early.

As you're building passive income streams, you're working smarter, not harder. You are choosing to create opportunities for more money to flow freely to you, whether you're actively working or not. Plus the magic about passive income is that this money gives you the financial freedom to improve the quality of your life, while giving you time to do what you want to do, without being chained to a 9-to-5 job you despise.

Now that you have a better understanding of what passive income is, let's talk about what it is not.

First, passive income is *not* always 100% passive. We've covered this before, but it bears repeating. With passive income, you will need to invest a little time or money, or both time and money. In most instances, you'll do something to keep the passive income coming in. Often not much work is required, but some is for sure. For instance, if your chosen passive income method is writing a blog, you will likely create fresh content, from time to time, so visitors keep visiting your blog, buying products you're selling, or clicking on ads. Or, if your preferred method is lending money to others, once those loans are paid off, you'll then choose more people to lend money to in order to continue earning passive income. Even with stocks, mutual funds, annuities, and bonds, you'll monitor and sell them as needed.

So get it out of your head that you won't do anything further once you set up your passive income streams.

Second, some passive income sources are actually semipassive and have an active component. An example of semipassive income is starting a freelance writing or graphic design business, and then hiring a team to complete all projects. As you can see, your contractors will do the actual work, but you will manage them and interact with clients. Although you have more freedom than a typical 9-to-5 job, income is dependent upon your contractors' efforts. Another example of semipassive income is someone who buys or rents a vending machine business. Not only will they be on call for any emergencies but they'll refill the machines and manage the contractors too.

Third, most passive income will require an initial investment of time to make it flow. For instance, you need money upfront to invest in stocks, annuities, CD ladders, and peer–to-peer lending. However, if you don't have any capital to invest, you will either find someone to invest for you or use another creative nonpassive method to make the money you need to invest. Here are some examples of low-cost but time-consuming methods:

- Writing and selling eBooks or trade publications.
- Designing and selling online courses (Udemy is a great platform).
- Taking incredible photos and selling them to royalty-free sites.
- Creating and selling T-shirts.
- Composing music, filming short videos, making arts and crafts projects, producing commercials, and then selling the rights.
- Creating an app.
- Starting an online sales and marketing network by partnering with a large multilevel or affiliate company.

<u>Note</u>: Whenever you invest in any passive-income method that requires a bit of upfront cash, do your research to make sure that the investment is sound before proceeding.

Ready to learn and earn?

I'm ready to teach you!

Passive Income Streams

1. Let's Get Started

Now that I've piqued your interest, you're probably getting excited about discovering new passive income streams. The good news is that finding streams that interest you aren't complicated at all. You are only limited by your creativity and imagination. Literally hundreds of ways can make you passive income, and many of them can be done using the Internet, a computer, and a cell phone.

You don't even have to make an upfront investment to get started. If capital is required, you can use other methods of passive income to make the capital you need and then reinvest it in the project that requires capital. For instance, if you need to make $500 to create a professional online store or website, you can use your phone or computer to watch videos to earn cash, and/or sell your online data to companies willing to pay for information, and/or use online shopping portals (for items you plan to buy anyway), and more. Once you have the $500, you can use it to create your online store/website.

The beauty of this plan is that you can get started today. It matters not if you're cash-strapped, and have limited time and capital. By being creative, you can make income today.

Now before we delve into the precise how-to steps of choosing your first passive-income method, let's take some time to create some passive-income goals. By figuring out what you want to achieve in the next three, six, nine, and twelve months, you'll be more likely to achieve your goals. When you set up your goals, don't just choose any goals. You need to write down SMART (specific, measurable, achievable, realistic, and time-bound) goals that clearly identify what goals you have for your future. For instance, my SMART passive-income goal for my eBook publishing stream is to make $3,500+ a month in passive income from the sale of twelve self-help eBooks by July 31, 2017. As you can see, my goal is specific, measurable, achievable (assuming I produce one book a month), realistic (I am fired up and can do it), and has a set date (my youngest son's birthday).

When you're creating your SMART passive-income goal, I want you to really think about how much money you want to achieve by the three, six, nine, and twelve-month marks. Think about how you'll make this money and whether it is realistic for you. Do you have a set date in mind? If so, good. You're on the right track.

For this next exercise, I want you to visualize yourself making this set amount of money from your passive income stream and feeling the freedom you have when you achieve this SMART goal. See yourself happier and more at peace, and buying the things you want without worry or fear. Really feel successful from the inside out.

Think about those things that have held you back in the past and what you will do to make sure these barriers don't restrict you. Be open and honest with yourself about how you'll overcome any negativity and self-doubt.

Make a commitment to work hard to achieve your SMART passive-income goals and to not let anyone or anything deter you from them. Commit to see each of your goals through, no matter how hard it is and how much you want to quit.

Keep in mind that you'll be tempted to give up at times. Don't. You're likely right on the cusp of succeeding, and, if you just stick it out a little while longer, you'll experience success.

Here are a few tips to keep you motivated toward success:

- **Don't allow others to confuse you**. Reflect on your SMART goals daily. Understand the reasons why you want passive income. Commit and recommit to make that money—no matter what.

- **Don't complicate your life all at once.** Take it slow and learn. Pace yourself. Work on one passive-income goal at a time, and, once set up and earning passive income, move on to the next one. Choose a goal that excites you.

- **Don't allow distractions to confuse you.** If you have questions, ask the right people, and don't be afraid to research the pros and cons of each passive-income project. Every successful passive-income venture started off somewhere. They didn't have all the answers, and neither will you. Check out our resource section, and get help when you need it.

- **Don't be afraid to make mistakes.** We're all human, and we all make mistakes. The best way is to learn from these mistakes and keep trying. By starting small, your mistakes will not be huge, and you can easily recover.

- **Don't be impatient.** Passive income takes time. And there will always be those naysayers who remain negative about passive income. Don't let their fears or angst get to you. If you believe in your passive-income plan, give it your best shot!

Commit right now to making this the best year ever!

It feels good to have a positive attitude and to make a commitment to your future, doesn't it? Commit right now. I'm proud of you.

Now that you are 100% committed and have listed your SMART goals and have gotten rid of any barriers to success, it's time to implement an action plan. You'll set yourself up for success by creating a realistic passive-income investment plan. Many people refer to it as a spending plan. With your spending plan, you'll list your discretionary income as well as any outgoing expenses. You'll include all income (after taxes) and subtract your fixed expenses, like child care, tuition, rent, mortgage and insurance, and varying other expenses, such as cell phone bills, utilities, groceries, eating out, etc. You'll then put aside no less than 10% of all income for emergencies.

Now look at the money left over. This money you will use to create passive income streams. This money will be invested in a passive-income account to make your passive-income dreams a reality. If you don't have any money for this account, you must trim those expenses until you have at least $10 a month to contribute (hopefully more)!

Once you have an amount in mind, set up a separate passive-income bank account at a bank or credit union. It doesn't matter if it's $10, $100, or $1,000 dollars—set it aside. Make a commitment that, anytime you get paid or receive income of any kind, first you'll put 10% of your income into your savings, and second you'll put this set-aside amount into your passive-income account.

Commit to only use the funds in the passive-income account for passive-income opportunities. Nothing else. Got it?

To give your passive-income bank account a bonus, sign up for a bank or credit union account that offers an initial sign-up offer. For instance, certain banks—like Chase Bank—offer $150 plus sign-up bonuses to new customers who open up a Chase Total Checking account. To sweeten the deal, Chase also offers a $100 bonus if you open up a savings account and a checking account. Of course you must deposit $10,000 into the savings account for ninety days, but it's still a sweet deal. And for those who set up both accounts, you get $250. Not a bad bonus, right? Remember that bank bonuses change from time to time so don't assume a bonus is still available. Be diligent about your research before signing up for any bonus. *Hint*: Doctor of Credit (http://www.doctorofcredit.com) is a great site to check for current bank bonuses. Also expect to receive a 1099 form at tax time, showing the bonus as income, so you'll owe taxes on that amount.

What's Next?

Now that we've set up our separate passive-income account, it's time to focus on generating passive income.

To appeal to everyone, I've broken down these methods into easy, medium, and harder, more complicated. Hopefully this will eliminate any fears and encourage you to start now. Plus each method can build on the other. For instance, if you need $100 capital, you can use a few easy methods to save up enough to invest in a medium-level method. Then, when you have generated enough money from easy-and medium-level methods, you can take those funds to invest in a harder, more complicated method. The point is to not let money stand in your way. Use the profits from previous passive income streams to create new ones.

Speaking of income, you may be wondering how much you can earn from passive income. I'm not going to lie to you. I don't know, as it depends on the persons, the method(s) they choose, and the effort they put forth. However, with the methods mentioned in this guide, you can make enough to quit your day job someday as you build financial freedom for your family.

You likely won't get rich overnight, but, with every passive income stream you create, you get closer and closer to your dream of financial independence. For instance, search engine toolbars that pay you for web searching can pay up to $10 a month. Website shopping portals, like Ebates can earn you up to $20 or more per shopping trip. Selling your online data could earn you $50 a month. Interest from peer-to-peer lending and bank accounts can earn $75 a month. Apps that allow you to watch videos for cash rewards could earn up to $100 a month. Creating your own app to sell to others could earn $250+. Having your own online store or website that sells products or promotes ads can earn you up to six figures a month.

The best part about passive income is that it is not limiting. You can use one method or you can use one hundred methods. The decision is really up to you.

Let's now take a look at these passive-income ideas. Feel free to try out the ones that resonate with you and ignore the ones that do not. Some of them have been around for a while, and some of them are relatively new. Every opportunity provided is a time-tested method to earn passive income. I've personally used each method and will continue to do so to reach my financial goals.

2. Easy-Peasy Methods

(No Prior Experience or Special Skills Required)

$10–$100+ a Month Club

The beautiful thing about this set of income opportunities is that they are free to start and typically yield about $10–$150 profit a month. In this section, you'll find some passive ideas and a few semipassive ones that require a little bit of activity from you at the beginning but are easily automated with minimal effort required. Although these methods won't necessarily make you a millionaire, they are a great way for you to start making passive income today so that you can later invest in other more lucrative methods.

Data-Selling

The first group of passive-income opportunities involves data-selling. More than ever, businesses are interested in gaining access to individuals' personal data so that these businesses can:

- Better understand their targets' needs.

- Market their business services or product offerings to these targets.

- Predict behavior, preferences, and habits of their targets.

- Improve the structure of each business's marketing campaigns and profit. By knowing this insider information, the businesses can avoid heavy losses from a "hit in the dark" marketing strategy.

- Pinpoint specific actions that would appeal to a specific group of people.

Now, you may be wondering what companies are willing to pay for information about people's addresses or general locations, income levels, genders, work histories, and family demographics. They're also willing to pay for info on the type of companies people promote on social media, how frequently they use their credit versus debit cards, amounts they typically spend online and off-line, buying habits, and other information as well.

Personal data is also known as "big data" because anyone who manages it holds a ton of sensitive information that companies want. Just imagine if a business had information about all the people who have Facebook accounts or who have traveled to Asia in the past ten years. That would be an enormous amount of data that could be sold to or used by interested parties, like big businesses.

For instance, companies like Nike have taken this concept a bit further with their apps. The Nike+ ecosystem app can store data about your exercise and fitness program. It even knows more about your heart's performance than you do when you are actively exercising. It uses what it knows to accurately time a shoe or exercise-gear ad right when you're in the exercising mood and uses this information as a strategic marketing gold mine. Ingenious, right?

Well, now you too can profit on this gold mine. You can sell your personal data to companies that want it. You can earn extra income and, more importantly, control who gets to use your personal information. You can even choose what information to sell so you don't feel overexposed and vulnerable.

Before you make the decision to sell or share your data, follow these simple rules:

- Investigate the site first and find out if it is legitimate.

- Never share private and financial information, just general data. You won't be asked to—and you shouldn't—give your exact address or social security number.

- Read the fine print in any agreement before joining to make sure you understand exactly what information you're selling and how much you'll be paid.

- Know the risks. Only partner with well-known and established companies that have secure encryption services built in to keep your data safe from hackers.

Some established websites that will pay you to share your data are Nielsen, AppOptix, Datacoup, Cross Media Panel, Media Insiders panel, and more. Now we will provide detailed information on each company and how to get started.

The Nielsen Mobile App – Data-Selling #1

Earning Potential: About $4.16 a month or $50 a year.

Time Required to Set Up: Less than twenty minutes, then it runs passively.

The Nielsen Mobile App offers another opportunity for users to earn up to $50 in gift cards each year, just for using their mobile device! After downloading the app on your mobile device (available for Android devices, Apple devices, and Kindle Fire), you just use your phone the way you always do.

The app collects data about how you use your phone, such as when and how often you play games or use various apps. Sensitive data on your device is not accessible to the app. While the app is running quietly in the background, you're collecting points that can ultimately be used to cash in on gift cards or electronics.

Joining Nielsen Mobile is easy. Just:

1. Consent to the Terms and Conditions of the Nielsen Privacy Policy.
2. Be over eighteen years of age.
3. Fill out the enrollment form found on the website.
4. Download the app on your mobile device.
5. Complete an online profile.

This app works with an Internet connection, which means you could incur charges for data transmission that Nielsen will not cover. A fair estimate of data usage connected to this app is about 2 MB.

When you join, Nielsen promises not to use any membership data for advertising or direct marketing. However, it will collect the following data:

- Your name, address, email, phone number, gender, age, location, annual income, educational attainment.
- Time stamps.
- Call history and duration.
- Hashed phone numbers.
- SMS, MMS, IM, email, even messages sent through or received via Bluetooth and Infrared.
- Notifications.
- Bluetooth data, like addresses and devices to which you are connected.
- IP address.
- Network information, traffic, and WLAN connections.
- System information (battery state, dock state, profiles, device ID, and settings).
- Use of GPS, apps, multimedia, and VPN state.
- Browsing activities.

The data collected will never be traceable back to you. This app only tracks the use of your devices and your location.

Payout for earnings is in the form of points, which can be converted to gift cards or electronic items, like DVD players, digital cameras, or TVs. Once you've received these gift cards, you can swap them at a gift card exchange, like Gift Card Granny, for cash.

Join Nielsen Mobile here: http://www.nielsen.com

AppOptix – Data-Selling #2

Earning Potential: About $4.16 a month or $50 a year.

Time Required to Set Up: The app can be up and running within minutes of downloading.

AppOptix is another research panel looking to purchase data on how you use your Android smartphone. <u>Note</u>: This is only for Android users. Unfortunately, if you're an Apple user, you're not eligible. This is another app which runs in the background. Depending on how much data they gather from your phone, you will get a certain number of points. These points can be exchanged for up to one $50 gift card from Amazon per year. The audience is limited, as are the rewards. However, if you do happen to match their criteria, you're in for a treat.

First, apply for membership. After you get approved, install the app and let it run in the background of your device as it collects data about how you use your device. It doesn't see or record the details of what you do within any application but rather just records when and for how long you use each application. Other sensitive data on your device is not accessed. For as long as the app is active on your device, you accumulate points that can be used to redeem up to $50 in Amazon gift cards each year.

AppOptix promises not to use or sell any personal identification information. They're not going to record or listen to your phone calls. Instead they gather some rather generic usage information from your phone.

- List of applications installed on the device.
- The name and launch periods of the applications, BUT application contents are not monitored.
- Time stamp and duration of the activities.
- The specifications of your device, such as what sensors are contained in it and when activated.
- The battery and network performance of your phone.

- The location of your device via GPS (if your device is so equipped).

This one is only open to Android users in the United States. Find the home page here and apply for membership here.

If you have an Android 5.0, you must agree to give AppOptix permission to run on your cell phone. This is not the case for other versions.

The steps to using AppOptix are simple:

1. Download the app.

2. Receive an email confirmation.

3. Complete the profile form. This automatically pays you one hundred points!

For every week the app runs on your Android, you get another one-hundred-point reward. Once you reach three hundred points, you can convert your points to a $10 Amazon gift card. However, every member can only be paid a maximum of $50 in gift cards for the year. For those of you who want cash, you can convert the gift cards to cash via a reputable gift-card exchange site like Card Pool, Gift Card Granny, or Raise.

A word of caution for those on a limited phone plan: this app runs continuously unless you shut down your phone, which means you could be using data and not know about it until your phone bill arrives.

Join AppOptix today!

https://panel.strategyanalytics.com/default.aspx?mod=faqs

Datacoup – Data-Selling #3

Earning Potential: About $8 and up monthly.

Time Required to Set Up: About thirty minutes to set up, then it runs passively.

Datacoup began as an aggressive New York start-up in 2014 and was one of the first to offer money to those willing to be data-mined. Today it is still going strong, and access to your data is limited to your social media accounts and transaction feeds from debit or credit cards. The company does not sell your personal identifying details. They remove any traces of who you are and simply sell your trends and Internet activities to companies.

This is a platform for you to connect with via many data sources. Data connections are easy and secure. You can connect banking information, debit and credit cards, online accounts—anything. Once you have all your accounts connected, a profile is built and will provide an overview of potential data. This data is then for sale for those looking for buyer groups, and, when your data has been bought, you will be notified and paid. You must have earned a $5 minimum before you are paid, and then you can have cash sent right to your account or any debit card you like.

To get started, visit their website (https://datacoup.com/) and start your profiling. This app is only available to US residents.

- Allow Datacoup access to your social media accounts.
- Connect your debit and credit cards for a one-time, read-only connection.
- Build your profile page.
- Agree to sell your personal data.

The money you earn can be accessed through Visa, MasterCard, or your debit card on designated payout dates—usually the end of the month. If your earnings reach $25, then it is put on hold until you redeem them, as the company does not allow payouts over $25. Once you have redeemed the $25, you can start earning again. To keep track of the money you are making, open your Data Profile. Here you will see your connections, Internet activities, and how activities (attributes) are ranked.

If someone buys your data, you will get an email notification. At present, Datacoup is buying the data, but the price of your data could increase if another company wants it. To earn more, you can also answer surveys, and participate in their beta testing and private conferences.

Website: http://www.datacoup.com

Screenwise Trends/Cross Media Panel – Data-Selling #4

Earning Potential: About $12+ a month (depending on the amount of devices).

Time Required to Set Up: Minutes after downloading and installing the app.

Cross Media Panel, which used to be Screenwise Trends, is Google's market research app. Its main goal is to gather data to improve Chrome, Android, and YouTube. Google has partners, which they refer to as Panel Partners, who can access your information to help them with their businesses.

You can use your desktop or mobile devices to install the app technology referred to as Meters. Anything you use that has Internet connections can have Meters, including game consoles, cable boxes, and tablets.

The information collected is limited to:

- Usage.
- Your content and the ads you view.
- Browsing and Internet activities.
- Browser settings, device ID, data usage, data from sensors.
- Operating systems and apps used.
- Time stamps on emails, phone calls, IM, SMS, or MMS, including any public information, like business names and phone numbers.

- Videos and shows watched.
- Music listened to, games played.
- Biometrics of device user, including location.
- Personal information you voluntarily provide.
- Screen content.
- Information stored in your devices.
- Cookies history.
- Use of Google products.

You can opt out of the tracking system by going on Guest mode, so Metering stops, but diagnostics continues. Under the app agreement, the device owner takes the responsibility of making sure anyone under the age of thirteen does not use the Metered devices without the adult owner's consent, and, if allowed, the minors must register as a Guest, or you must register your minors with the app so they can sign in under a non-Metering mode. As the device owner, it is also your responsibility to inform any person using your Metered devices that it has a tracking app.

Google also admits to getting information from third parties about you as part of their research, although they do not do it regularly.

To get started, do this:

1. Register.
2. Install the Chrome browser add-on.
3. Start browsing the web or using your device.

This app is only available for US residents and can be installed only by adults (defined as eighteen years old and older).

The app will immediately start tracking your Internet searches. You can add it to any device you may use or even install an app for mobile web searching. Then you go about your everyday searches and get paid for it. Signing up is free and usually takes about fifteen minutes. You can get up to $6 as a sign-up bonus and $3 weekly; most rewards are offered in gift-card form.

Cross Media Panel will stop accepting new registrants at a certain limit. However, they regularly reopen for registration. So, if you can't get in now, check again after a few days.

Website: https://www.crossmediapanel.com/

Media Insiders Panel – Data-Selling #5

Earning Potential: An active user can expect to earn around $15 per month.

Time Required to Set Up: None, other than the initial time required to set up an account. After the installation of the app, this app will run passively.

Media Insiders is an application available for Android, Apple, and PC devices that runs in the background and collects data on your usage, much like Nielsen Mobile and AppOptix. To put it bluntly, they spy on you. To their credit, they are up-front about this so-called espionage. A research foundation runs it, and researching devices are used. The app captures and measures every activity, including sharing, viewing, clicking, chatting, downloading, listening to the TV shows you watch, web pages visited, videos watched, ads viewed, and even your every move on social media (Facebook, Twitter), and more. If you're okay with this, then, by all means, download the app.

Media Insiders is operated and managed by Symphony Advanced Media, a media analyst company based in San Francisco that collects data from its research in order to help brands understand their market better.

Four kinds of rewards can be earned with Media Insiders:

- Cash-out via PayPal.

- Donations to charities.
- Gift cards.
- Sweepstakes entries.

To earn points, use your devices to do ordinary activities, like search the Net; watch or stream videos, films, and TV shows; or listen to music. On rare occasions, the company may also send you the occasional survey to fill out.

Media Insiders Panel is a perfect opportunity for individuals who don't have sensitive information on their phone. However, you must meet the following requirements:

- US resident with a valid email address.
- At least thirteen years old.
- Own an Android device version 4.0 or greater but not rooted and/or Kindle Fire HD devices with built-in microphone.
- Pass the initial Media Insiders' survey.
- Agree to the terms and conditions of Media Insiders.
- Download the program and initiate using your email address.

If this sounds like something you're interested in, fill out some basic information about yourself and your devices. You must allow the app access to your app history, photos, multimedia files, location, call information, device information, camera, and microphone.

You will also be asked about your social media accounts and requested to synch them to the app.

Once the app is active, your points will accumulate until you choose to cash-out for gift cards to many different national and international retail stores, or receive $25 PayPal cash.

You will need at least 500 points to claim your reward of a $5 gift card, and, if you choose to let the points build to 2,500, you qualify for a $25 PayPal payout.

In addition, by simply allowing the app to run on your device, you qualify to join the sweepstakes with a weekly draw of $25, a monthly draw of $100, and a quarterly draw worth $10,000.

Media Insiders Panel allows you to have up to three devices per account running passively. The idea is, if you have more devices, you can get more rewards. The real question is this: Why would they pay you merrily for running their app? What does their app do? Both are excellent questions. I leave it to you to find the answers and to decide if this works for you.

To get started, there is a registration survey. Complete the survey, then download the app. Activate the app, and you're all done.

Join Media Insiders today!

Website: https://www.mediainsiders.com/

3. Online Shopping Portals

($10–$100+ a Month Club)

Required Earning Potential: About $15 a month or more, depending on how often you use the portals.

Time Required to Set Up: Five minutes to sign up; five minutes to click a link to partnered sites.

Websites, such as Ebates and TopCashback, act as shopping portals, and they earn commissions when you purchase products from stores listed on their websites. A percentage of each commission is then shared with you. As the cost of living rises, you spend more out of pocket for necessary household items. Estimates show the average US household spends approximately $6,759 annually just on food. These online shopping-portal sites are a great way to obtain passive income in return for things you'd buy anyway.

Ebates and TopCashback are two of my favorite online portals. Here's a description of how they work:

Ebates – Online Shopping Portal #1

Ebates allows you to shop at over two thousand stores, including Macy's, Walmart, Kohl's, Aéropostale, Amazon, Bath & Body Works, and the list goes on and on. The amount of rebate money received from shopping varies at these stores. They claim that you can earn as much as 40% cash back on some purchases. Also over ten thousand coupons and promotional codes can be used at the same time.

When you become a member of Ebates, you will receive hundreds of exclusive coupon offers and up to 25% cash back on all purchases. There is no cost to join. In addition, if you refer a friend, you will receive a $5 bonus for each friend who joins and makes a qualifying purchase. This purchase must be greater than $25. With each friend who signs up for Ebates, you will be entered into a giveaway.

To use the portal, you can visit the Ebates site directly, download the mobile app, or use the Ebates Cash Back button/toolbar, downloadable to most browsers. If you prefer to use the mobile app or the website, you basically search for the store you'd like to visit, click the offer, and then activate it. Or you can use the toolbar add-on that alerts you when cash-back opportunities are available.

With the toolbar/cash-back add-on, you visit an eligible partner store, and a pop-up appears and tells you to activate the cash-back offer. If the offer is not activated, the button (on your toolbar) flashes red; however, when you activate the offer, it turns green. Whenever the offer is activated, your identifying information is automatically entered so that you receive credit for the "shopping trip." In addition, if any coupons or promotional codes are available, you should enter them as well and receive further discounts.

Keep in mind, if you activate the Ebates offer, buy something from one site, and then visit another site, you'll only receive credit for the first shopping trip unless you activate the offer again.

Once you start earning rewards, they will show as pending in your account within a few hours or more. However, some stores take up to thirty days to receive your rewards. There are several ways to get paid. You can have a check sent to you, only mailed out every three months (May 15, August 15, November 15, and February 15). You can check your balance via the mobile app or the website.

You must have a balance of $5.01 or greater to receive your payout money. If less than this amount is in your account, your rewards will be carried over to the next period. If you choose this pay-by-check method, it is important to keep all your information up to date to ensure that the check is sent to the correct address. You can also choose to have your money sent to PayPal. Your PayPal account must be verified in order to receive payment, and said payments are on the same three-month schedule as the check option. You can also opt to have your money sent to a charity or family member. Go to your account settings and input the information on where your money should go. Ebates will not validate tax-deductible donations.

Website: http://www.ebates.com/

TopCashback – Online Shopping Portal #2

TopCashback is another cash-back portal open to residents of the United States and Canada, and claims to give you the highest cash-back reward out of all online portals. According to them, they have a 100% cash-back policy, where members get 100% of all cash-back commissions paid, and TopCashback doesn't charge administrative fees.

TopCashback earns income through advertising banners and additional deals with individual stores. Occasionally they receive bonuses from companies for certain promotions.

They have over 3,500 partner stores, places like Bloomingdale's, Walmart, Amazon, and many more. TopCashback also offers free shipping, and extra instant-money-off discounts and coupons. You can also refer friends and family to join and receive a bonus. Your referral must meet a payable status, and their email addresses must be authenticated. You will receive a $15 cash-back payout once your referrals meet this site's requirements.

It can take up to two months for the cash to be paid to you because invoices are sent at the end of the month. Afterward the stores will send payment to TopCashback, and then the rebate is put in your shopping-portal account. Once the money is available there, you can request a payout immediately. However, you must wait for quarterly payouts.

To request a payout, simply go to your TopCashback account and click on the Payout button. Here you will see the various payout options and the amount available. Click on the Payable button and choose the method of payout. If you want your money sent to your bank account, it may take up to four working days before it reaches your account. You can also have your money sent to PayPal (this method happens almost instantly) as long as your PayPal account is verified. However, the verification process could take four working days to occur.

Website: https://www.topcashback.com/

4. Getting Paid to View Ads by Online Reward Companies

Easy-Peasy

($100+ a Month Income Club)

An online reward company is a company that pays users to perform certain actions. Typically individuals can earn points from referrals, sharing and posting about products, staying subscribed to each company's website, and filling out membership forms. In addition, individuals are paid for viewing advertisements from companies that might interest them.

But why would advertisers use online reward companies to lure prospects? Short answer: advertising works.

Individuals who view ads via online reward companies are more likely to buy the product advertised, and to tell their friends and family about such a product as well (assuming the product meets their needs and the product's marketing hits all their hot buy-it-now, gotta-have-it buttons). These companies are smart and use these ads to reach customers, near and far, in a quick and effective way. Pairing with online reward companies makes this happen.

In short, by appealing to their target audience and putting their message in front of the right people at the right time, these businesses can increase profits tremendously. By using the Internet to connect with their target audience (who happens to be on reward company sites), they can test ad effectiveness and find customers who want the businesses' products and services. Other company benefits include:

- Obtaining immediate responses compared to traditional advertising methods.
- Keeping costs low as they evaluate different types of ads.

- Matching with an existing subscriber base, so it's mostly a matter of companies marketing to a particular online reward system that has their target members.

- Tracking responses through the online reward portal.

And users benefit by making money viewing ads. The users can also find quality products and services they might not know about and can pass on the word to others. Plus companies will likely continue to partner with these online-reward users and pay even more in advertising in upcoming years.

According to a study by Pew Research Center, last year digital advertising increased by 40%, and, in the next four years, it should overtake all other forms of advertising and promotions. Wow! When you think about all the companies with exceptionally large budgets and willingness to splurge on digital advertising, you realize that the potential to make money is there. So let's get your piece of the advertising pie.

Here's how to make passive income by pairing with these online reward companies.

Swagbucks – Online Reward Company #1

Earning Potential: About $4–$5 a day or more; about $120–$150 per month.

Time Required to Set Up: Varies, but you typically leave your phone and computer on for eight or more hours while you complete other tasks.

Swagbucks is a California-based online rewards company with an A+ rating with the BBB. This company enables users to earn money by performing certain actions. Swagbucks offers several unique opportunities for making passive income, including watching ads, TV shows or movie clips, shopping online, using grocery store coupons; and receiving cash back using their Swagbucks links, using their coupon-finder at the grocery store, or using the Swagbucks search engine. Whenever you successfully perform these actions, you are immediately awarded Swagbucks, which can be "cashed out" for PayPal cash or gift cards. Periodically you can purchase gift cards at a discount when Swagbucks runs a sale, and they often run challenges where you can join teams to earn additional Swagbucks too.

You can also add the Swagbucks button (SwagButton) via Chrome or Firefox, and, when you shop at your favorite online stores, you can earn Swagbucks (SB) as well, assuming you activate SB Cash Back.

Swagbucks are worth $0.01 each, and it takes 550 points for the $5 PayPal gift card. Although $0.01 might not seem like a lot initially, those daily pennies can add up, and you can make upward of $150 or more per month for smart Swagging.

Some individuals (including yours truly) use cheap burner Android phones purchased with a Swagbucks redemption (a Best Buy gift card). Other people use a burner iPhone. **Using your primary phone is not recommended.**

Once you have a burner phone, download Swagbucks TV and Swagbucks-partnered mobile apps from the Google Play store or App Store.

These include Swagbucks TV, EntertaiNow, Lifestylz.tv, Sportly.tv, IndyMusic.tv, and MovieCli.ps, as they all allow you to earn 10 SB a day per app. The Swagbucks and Swagbucks TV apps require that Android users have Version 4.1 or later. For those who run iPhones, iPods, or iPads, these devices must have iOS 8.0 or later in order to run Swagbucks, but iOS Version 7.0 or later to run Swagbucks TV.

Once the apps have been downloaded, log into the Swagbucks site or the app and get started. Each video you watch will play for thirty seconds to two minutes, and a couple of ads may play afterward. Sometimes you will also be eligible for bonus rounds where you can earn more. Then, while they are playing, you can run Swagbucks TV via the SwagButton or directly from their site and earn up to 150 more SB a day. You typically must watch ten videos to earn two Swagbucks. You can leave the videos running while you do other computer tasks, however. Keep in mind that you can only win 150 SB a day from exclusively watching videos on your computer, but, when you combine that amount with the SB earned via the mobile apps, your passive income grows.

By running these short videos on your burner phone and computer, you can earn $3–$4 of passive income a day. While $3–$4 a day may not seem like much, it is still $90–$120 a month more than you had. This extra money can fund other start-up costs for income streams with higher returns, like a blog with revenue-generating ads.

Now, before you buy a boatload of phones to "get your Swag on," keep in mind that these apps sometimes freeze, and there are some limitations to earning Swagbucks. I have never gotten suspended for running one burner phone a day and using a spare computer to run Swagbucks TV, but your individual mileage may vary. So tread lightly.

Here are a few bonus tips:

1. Switch your search engine over to the Swagbucks engine, which you can do by visiting Settings on your Chrome or Firefox browser. For Chrome, click on Settings from the drop-down list, select Manage Search Engines, and look for Swagbucks under Other Search Engines to make it your default. To default your search engine in Firefox, go to your browser search field (at the right of your address bar), click the drop-down menu, and look for Swagbucks. Click on it, and Swagbucks is now your default search engine.

    If you prefer not to make Swagbucks your default, you can simply use their search engine at the top of their home page. Every time you do a search, you will automatically earn Swagbucks without even trying. Sometimes you will even hit bonus rounds, though they are rare.

    Download and use the SwagButton, an add-on in Chrome and Firefox which allows you to watch videos, enter SB codes, and shop. With the shopping feature, you will also be notified if a store you are visiting is a Swagbucks partner, and you can then click on it via the Swagbucks link for extra points. For instance, Walmart offers 7 SB per dollar spent; Walgreens and Target currently offer 2 SB per dollar spent.

2. Make use of the Swagbucks coupons. For every grocery coupon you print and use, you will save money on essential items plus earn 10 SB.

3. Plan to fill your Daily Goal Meter each day. Every day you visit Swagbucks, the Daily Goal Meter displays a Swagbucks earning goal based on your personalized earning behavior. If you reach that goal, you will receive a bonus. Even better, if you hit enough of these goals in a row, you will receive a streak bonus in addition to your daily bonus. The longer your streak is, the bigger the rewards will be. For instance, when you hit your goal for seven days, you get a bonus of twenty SB; for fourteen days, one hundred SB; for twenty-one days, two hundred SB; and for thirty days, three hundred SB.

   Be aware that the daily bonus gets higher every day, so initially it may be thirty SB and the next day fifty SB—but you must claim the bonus at the beginning of the next month in order to receive credit for it. If I'm not mistaken, you have fifteen to sixteen days after the end of the month to claim it. So, if you receive a bonus in July, you have until August 15 or 16 to claim the previous month's bonus.

4. Plan to hit your maximum video earnings each day on your computer and mobile device. You can even run Swagbucks at work on your mobile phone—just make sure you have unlimited Wi-Fi and that your boss does not prohibit this. When you hit your goals, you get a bonus. For instance, when you hit your goal for seven days, you get a bonus of twenty SB.

5. When you cash-out your earnings via PayPal or via a store gift card, you can use the funds to buy more inexpensive devices to run Swagbucks or other apps on, which we'll discuss later.

Happy Swagging!

To get started, go to http://www.swagbucks.com/refer/noone2das.

Perk TV – Online Reward Company #2

Earning Potential: About $6 a day or $180 a month—with four devices running Perk TV app ($4 per day), one phone running Perk Pop Quiz ($1 per day), and one computer running Perk TV videos ($1 a day).

Time Required to Set Up: Varies, but you typically leave on your phone, computer, and/or other devices for eight or more hours while you complete other tasks.

The Perk TV app gives you points for using your iPod, tablet, or phone to run videos and ads. Perk TV is truly a passive source of income. With Perk, simply set up your account, watch ads from your computer, or download the app. You then earn Perk Points and Perk Tokens. The difference between tokens and points is that their tokens can be redeemed for rewards, such as gift cards, electronics, charity donations, and PayPal Cash or Perk Plastik (a prepaid Discover card). Perk Points can only be used to enter any Perk sweepstakes and to be cashed in for tokens.

If you decide to cash-out to your Perk Plastik prepaid card, the redemptions are as follows:

- 1,100 points for $1.
- 2,200 points for $2.
- 5,500 points for $5.
- 11,000 points for $10.

You can also redeem your Perk Points for store gift cards or PayPal cash.

If you really want to maximize your earning potential, use one to four burner tablets, Androids, iPhones, or a combination of the above. These burner phones, tablets, and iPhones shouldn't cost you more than $15–$30 apiece, and they don't have to be connected with a phone plan. A prepaid phone (with Wi-Fi, but you won't activate the phone's Wi-Fi) will work perfectly for this purpose. Therefore, a wireless network (at work or at home) with unlimited Wi-Fi will be required. If you're worried about the electricity costs of using all these devices— don't. The average cost to run a Perk phone farm is between $0.50–$1 per year for a phone and approximately $2.50 per year for an iPad.

Any phone or tablet you use should be dedicated to Perking and must be compatible with the current version of the app. For instance, your burner phone or tablet must use Android 4.0.3 and up. To run Perk TV on an iPhone or iPod/iPad, iOS 7.0 or later is required. These phones can be purchased new from Best Buy, Amazon, Target, Walmart, or any other source, like eBay or Craigslist. Initially you should start off with one or two, and then build up your burner phone farm as you go along.

If you also want to run Perk on your Mac or Windows-based computer, this is possible as well. You simply log in the Perk website and watch videos through their site. In my experience, any updated computer with a reliable Internet connection should work.

Once you have your burner phones or tablet, download the Perk TV app from the Google Play store or App Store. Next, set up an account, and log in. Now set the app on low-bandwidth mode. If you choose not to download the app, you can still watch videos directly at http://www.perktv.com. For every video and ad that plays in the background, you will earn points. These points can then be redeemable for cash on your Perk Plastik Discover card or gift cards; the choice is yours. The beautiful thing about this is that it requires very little user interaction. Every few hours a pop-up will appear, asking if you are still watching. Just click Okay and leave it be until the next pop-up. Sometimes these pop-ups don't appear at all, and sometimes they appear several times a day.

While you won't become a millionaire or derive a full-time income using the Perk TV method, several people using Perk TV on old Android devices earn about $9 per week per device. As long as you don't pay several hundred dollars for the Android or iPhone device on top of a monthly limited data plan, the income should pay for the device within a month or two.

Note: Sometimes the app might crash and must be restarted, and occasionally you'll need to close an ad, but, otherwise, the videos will play (and earn) continuously without any further action from you.

You can supposedly have up to five devices per account with Perk. However, I typically only use two or three (as many people have reported being banned for using more than this number).

That means you can safely have one to five devices running Perk TV in the background in your home, earning about $18–17 per week.

You can do more with Perk if you want to earn points faster. If you log into your account on their website, you can always watch more videos to earn more points. Keep in mind, however, that Perk apps and websites don't always work seamlessly. Some days they work perfectly and other days not so much. On days when they don't work so well, you can use another moneymaking app (like CheckPoints instead).

Bonus Tips

1. You can also use Perk's Internet search function at Perk.tv to earn additional Perk points.

2. Since Perk allows family members to have more than one account per household, each with one to five devices, your family income can increase if family members set up separate accounts under the same IP and are willing to provide Perk with verifiable government IDs.

3. An app called Perk Pop Quiz is semipassive. With this one, you must interact with it from time to time by answering questions. Many people put it in lightning mode so the videos and ads appear faster. However, you must interact with it at least every hour. Although you are allowed to have five phones that also use Perk Pop Quiz, numerous people have been banned with this amount so it is best to only use one to two on Pop Quiz and only one to four on Perk TV.

4. Be careful about getting banned. One can be banned on Perk for a few reasons, including creating more than one account, fraudulent referrals, using a proxy IP address/VPN, using ad-blocking software, completing offers with fraudulent or fake information, using fast-forward applications, creating a bot or hack to exploit the Perk app or products, and using the app in a country where Perk is not available.

   If a Perk account has been canceled or banned, the accountholder should email Perk Support and ask why. Most of the online information available states that Perk will usually require the person to email or send in a state or government ID to prove identity, and the account should be reactivated.

5. To obtain the Perk Plastik Discover card, you must apply and then download the Perk Wallet to keep track of your account information. Note: Only two fees are associated with the card. If you request to have a written statement sent to you, there is a $7 charge. If your card is lost, a replacement card will cost $4.50. The card requires no credit checks, and the minimum age requirement is eighteen.

   After receiving your card, go to the Perk Wallet app and tap the Activate Card option in the menu and follow the instructions. To load money onto the card, go to the app. Select Manage Card and then Add Money. Your Perk Points will then be converted into cash and added to your card. A limit of $25 a day can be loaded to the card, and the total balance on the card cannot exceed $1,000.

   The card can be used anywhere in the United States where Discover is accepted. It can also be used online to pay bills and shop.

For: IOS and Android devices
Cost: Free

Website: www.getperk.com

Apps: http://www.perk.com/apps

More information about Perk: https://www.reddit.com/r/perktv/

5. Selling Your Creative Talents

(via eBooks, Blogging, Selling Photos, etc.)
Intermediate-to-Advanced Skills Required
($100+ a Month Club)

If you're like most smart investors, you realize that putting your funds into a bank account and hoping for the best isn't the most viable option for everyone. After all, to enjoy a $1,000+ monthly passive income stream from interest alone, you need at least $250,000 in active investments based on at least a 5% interest rate. This reality prompts many Americans (and others) to start saving early and to start saving more and more money to amass this $250,000 figure (or another figure of your choosing). Planning ways to source additional income while still part of the workforce is helpful. Passive income is a great way to make this happen.

If you're creative, you can use those intermediate-to-advanced talents to increase your passive income in literally hundreds of ways, like:

- Creating eBooks and POD books.
- Creating online classes.
- Monetizing your blog.
- Outsourcing.
- Affiliate and network marketing.
- Email marketing.
- Designing and selling T-shirts.
- Selling your photos.
- Starting your own YouTube channel.

- Crowdfunding.

- Peer-to-peer lending.

- High-interest banking.

- Credit card rewards.

Your passive income opportunities are only limited by your imagination. Here's a bit more detail about the ideas mentioned above.

6. Writing eBooks and Print-on-Demand Books

Earning Potential: Varies, depending on the price of each book and the number of copies sold.

Time Required: Thirty or more days to write the book (nonfiction or fiction); two or more hours to upload each to CreateSpace, Amazon, or another online platform.

In this technologically advanced era, self-publishing has become a way for authors to bypass the traditional publishing process and publish their own work. Authors are now publishing eBooks on Amazon and print-on-demand books on CreateSpace and other platforms. These books can cover a wide range of nonfiction and fiction genres, enabling authors to develop a profitable passive income stream.

The great news is you don't even need to be an established author or graphic designer to create your book. If you have no writing skills or simply hate writing, you can hire a ghostwriter to draft the book per your instructions and notes/outline. Then you can revise the draft as needed before sending it to a proofreader to make sure everything flows well. But you still must read and approve of the final product before uploading it online.

If you have no drawing skills (whether by hand or by computer), you can hire a graphic designer to create your cover. Heck, you can even hire a marketing consultant to market your book if you have no interest in doing so. Keep in mind the costs of hiring these individuals to assist you. Many indie authors who write their own content will typically pay $500+ for an eBook cover, promotional ads, editing/proofreading, and conversion services. However, an individual who needs a ghostwriter plus all the above will pay over $1,500 for a fifty-page book. Of course, if you have one or more of these skills, the costs will be minimized.

The writing process can be daunting, but the publishing process is not hard. Once you have a properly formatted book and have written your online description, you can typically submit your book to Amazon and CreateSpace and be published within forty-eight hours (assuming they approve of your content).

For any new authors uploading to Amazon, I would suggest pricing your book around $0.99–$2.99. You can always increase this once you've built a following. If you enroll in KDP Select, you'll have the option to run your book for free for five days or have a Kindle Countdown Deal. A Kindle Countdown Deal allows authors to run time-based deals that display the original price and a lower price that goes up with time. Amazingly you keep your original royalty rate during the Kindle Countdown deal, regardless of the new lower pricing.

For instance, if your book is regularly priced at $5.99, but your Kindle Countdown Deal price is $1.99, you'll still receive a 70% royalty on books sold, even at the lower price. This is huge, considering that you would only receive a 35% royalty rate on any books originally priced under $2.99.

In contrast, during your free KDP Select days, your enrolled books will be free. You will receive rankings against other free Kindle books and will revert back to paid Kindle status after the promotional period has ended. Many authors use this free book offering to attract new readers and to boost sales of their other books.

As previously mentioned, Amazon has two royalty structures—70% and 35%.

The 70% royalty program forces you to sell your eBook for at least $2.99 and the eBook pricing must be at least 20% lower than its physical counterpart. If you do not have any physical books for sale on Amazon, the 70% royalty option is the way to go, although with the KDP Select option, you are limited to only selling your selected and enrolled eBooks on Amazon for each ninety-day renewable period.

Websites: Amazon (https://kdp.amazon.com/) and Createspace (https://www.createspace.com/)

Regardless of whether you have books in KDP Select or not, the 70% royalty option allows you to make approximately $2 on every sale of a book priced at $2.99, which is the lowest pricing figure allowed under the 70% royalty option. The 35% royalty program allows you to have more say in how your price your book, as you can start your price point at $0.99.

One of the first things you should do is browse the Amazon Kindle marketplace. Look at the top sellers, and check out their reviews and book descriptions. Get a feel for what fiction genre or nonfiction topic sells and what doesn't.

If you are primarily interested in writing nonfiction, search to see how many nonfiction books make it to the Top 10. Next, look at what genre they belong to (like, self-help, a huge category) and what their main topic is (like, gaining self-esteem, a more defined group within the self-help books), plus what their covers look like. Also look at the average price of a Kindle nonfiction best seller and how many reviews they have and what their ratings are. These things will help you find your nonfiction niche and determine how much competition you'll have.

For example, when I last checked the self-help genre (within Amazon Kindle's eBooks), Amazon has designated eleven subgenres within this main category. The biggest subcategory, self-esteem, has 10,347 books online. The smallest subcategory, inner child, has 451 books online. So, if you write about your reader's inner child (or something related to this subgenre), you'll have less competition than if you were to write about your reader's self-esteem. Regardless, write what you desire but realize where the marketplace is at too.

Once you have defined your nonfiction niche, start writing. After your book is written, make sure to edit your manuscript or have someone else edit same to catch any grammar, spelling, organizational mistakes. Create an eye-catching cover and publish to Kindle. After publication, you may want to look into ways to market your book and get your name out there. Promotional sites—like Bargain Booksy, BookBub, bookSCREAM, Free Kindle Books and Tips, Reading Deals, Robin Reads, etc.—are some incredible ways to promote your work. Their prices range from $10 and up for a promotional ad that goes to their eBook readers, looking for great books at an affordable price.

Bargain Booksy (https://www.bargainbooksy.com)

This is a great first-timer's site for boosting book sales if you are an author planning to discount your book or already have it priced between $0.99 and $5. Free books are not accepted on this website; however, they are accepted at their sister site, Free Booksy. In contrast, Bargain Booksy is perfect for authors who are open to selling their books at a discount. This site has it all, from fiction to nonfiction, seasoned authors to the newest of the new. Plus you can feature one book per month. You can test your luck with the deal of the day or choose the bulk option to get your book out there in front of eager readers. Whatever your needs, this site is for you.

BookBub (https://www.bookbub.com/partners/author-profile)

This site allows you to reach many different e-reader platforms, not just Kindle like some other promotional sites. This community of readers is somewhat small, but this site is unique in that you can create an author profile and have readers follow you. This will allow readers to know when you are releasing new material, and help increase your sales and growth. Readers will be notified via email of your activity, and they can choose to follow you to continue getting updates. It is a unique approach to matching authors and prospective buyers without running through the streets, promoting yourself until your voice is lost.

bookSCREAM (http://bookscream.com/authors.php)

This is another Kindle-only website; however, as of July 18, 2016, it is accepting "book hints free of charge." This is their BETA phase of the system, and they expect to charge a nominal $1 fee for each book you want to promote in their newsletter. Their audience is small—only thirty thousand members—but this might be an easy way to get in on the ground floor of something that might turn huge. However, I think you'll have more success with other FREE sites out there. This may be a good time to let the first and second versions of this bookSCREAM site work out their bugs before you look to join.

Free Kindle Books and Tips (http://fkbt.com)

As indicated by the name of the website itself, this is strictly for Kindle users. Although it has a limited audience, it claims to have a community of over 675,000 members. If you are an author looking to boost your Kindle sales, all you must do is enter your email address, and they will notify you about ways to be added to their announcement list and named within blog posts reaching their large community. Your book must have at least four out of five stars on Amazon before it will be reviewed and potentially mentioned.

Reading Deals (http://readingdeals.com/submit-ebook)

The terms of this website are very clear if you want to submit your book for review. Make sure to follow this strict set of editorial guidelines, including length, grammar, cover, formatting, etc. Your book also has to be at least 33% off the normal price or free. They boast a community that streamlines the process of getting the books the readers want into their hands faster. Daily emails are sent to their audience, and your book could be featured in one of those emails. The ease of submission makes this a great site to start off your book promotion.

Robin Reads (http://robinreads.com/author-signup)

This key piece of information is important: Robin Reads is only available for people who have an Amazon account. This restricts your target audience, but the site boasts a growing community of over 120,000 hungry readers just waiting to get their hands on the next great novel. Once you submit your work, it goes through a review process, and is put on their site to begin boosting your book sales and promoting your title! In order to submit, you can try for the Premium Featured Slot Promotion, but, if you aren't selected for that, you can submit your work under one of the regular genre categories.

Other Marketing Methods

Other great marketing methods include book tours and social media marketing via Twitter, FB, and Instagram. You can also use online book tours, guest blogging, and more to get the word out there and to increase your passive income from your book sales.

7. Creating Udemy Online Courses

Earning Potential: Varies, depending on the popularity of the course and the number of students taking it.

Time Required: Varies, depending on the length of the course.

Do you like sharing your knowledge with others? Do you like creating content that will help others learn and grow? If so, creating Udemy courses is a tried-and-true method to make passive income while improving the lives of students, one at a time.

Here are some tips for creating your very first Udemy Course. The initial step is to pick a subject or niche in which you are an expert. This material should be something you feel comfortable discussing in great detail, especially if you are charging a fee for your course. The subject matter can be anything from the arts to earth and space sciences or even how to build an effective résumé. Once you have a topic, the next step is to create a course, featuring instructional videos, assignments, quizzes, follow-up materials, and so on. By uploading various teaching methodologies, you enable every student to learn in their own predominant style (visual, auditory, or kinesthetic).

Udemy is a great starting point for anyone wanting to hone their teaching skills and to learn the ins and outs of teaching on an online platform. The requirements to create a course and the barriers to instructor entry are extremely low. Once you've decided on a subject and created the materials needed for your course, you'll set the pricing. This is where things can get a little confusing if you've never set up a course before. Some instructors choose to make their first few course offerings free in hopes to gain a following of students. Once an instructor gains some notoriety, asking a nominal fee is almost understood. For someone new with no ratings, it's wise to set a lower price, around $10–$15. The lower price will continue to encourage a steady student base, which will in turn cause more people to sign up for your course, especially while the price is affordable.

Once you have created your course and uploaded it, expect to do some marketing before the passive income will start rolling in. Although Udemy does promote courses via sitewide discount days, you shouldn't rely on Udemy to do all of your marketing for you. Instead, your marketing methods should be specifically tailored to your targeted audience. For instance, free giveaways, course incentives, quizzes, follow-ups, and reviews are all valuable tools when building your credibility as an instructor. You can even start marketing with Facebook, Twitter, your own website, and so on. Your mission should be to recruit fifty to sixty students who do the marketing for you. In fact, once students take your courses, you can create spin-off courses to keep them coming back for more.

Don't be afraid to ask students for feedback. Reviews are extremely important for building your credibility as an online instructor. Not only will feedback help you improve current and future course offerings, but it will help you grow and refine future courses as well.

Who knows? With a little hard work and some creative self-marketing, you could turn a hobby into a successful career. Some Udemy instructors can earn anywhere from $500 to over $10,000 a month! If you're willing to put in the work, the profit potential can be huge with this passive income method!

Website: https://www.udemy.com/

8. Blogging for Cash

Just about everyone has a blog these days, from stay-at-home moms to corporate executives working for Fortune 500 companies. Blogging is in. It's not only a great way to share your knowledge and your passion but it is extremely fun and can be quite profitable as well. If you've been considering getting started, now is the time to do so.

Here are some tips and strategies:

Step 1: Know Your Target Audience

Who will be reading your blog? Is it going to be primarily young moms? Parents? Sports enthusiasts? How old are they? Do you expect more male or female readers or a combination of both? What type of content will they be searching for? Knowing your target audience is critical to having a successful blog and getting others to read what you write.

Step 2: Decide What Platform to Use

Most individuals start with WordPress, as it is extremely newbie-friendly and has all kinds of plug-ins to make your blogging experience easier. However, there are other options. With WordPress, you can use their web software and host it on your own domain-name site, or you can use Wordpress.org and use their platform. Either option is a great choice; however, it is typically best to have your blog on your own domain-name site so that you have greater control.

If maintaining control doesn't matter to you, you can use the popular alternative Blogger. It's very simple to use, but you cannot monetize (make any money from) your blog if you use Blogger. Blogger is backed by Google and is reliable and trustworthy. This platform makes the setup easy and takes you through the process step by step. There are many customization options, and you can purchase templates from other websites as well.

Another option is Tumblr. This platform is free; however, it does have less customization than some of the other options. The designs are simplistic, and it is a great place for new bloggers to start.

Finally, Live Journal is a great site for blogging, journaling, or keeping a diary. Note: It is always best to have your own blog connected to your own domain name.

Step 3: Create an Aesthetically Pleasing Website

WordPress has a wide variety of themes and templates to choose from, making your blog look good and making it easy to just plug in what you want. Remember that white space is important in setting up your blog. Your site should not be too cluttered. In addition, your blog should:

- **Utilize a nice array of color.** Choose colors for your website carefully. Test out different color palettes to see what is more aesthetically pleasing for you and your readers. White space is not simply wasted or empty space. It is the element around the page layout and design. It enhances readability and prioritizes content.

- **Include royalty-free images.** Make sure that the images you choose to place on your website are relevant and add value to your website.

- **Have textual content.** Populate your website with keyword-rich content. Use headings and subheadings to organize your website and make it easy to do a quick visual scan of what you are offering.

- **Be easy to navigate.** The easier it is for visitors to use your site, the better they will like it. Add things like a search function, side categories, footers, navigation buttons, and whatever else you think will make your site more user-friendly.

Websites: Wordpress (https://wordpress.org/),

Tumblr (https://www.tumblr.com/)

and Live Journal (http://www.livejournal.com/)

Step 4: Conduct Keyword Research

Keyword research is a search engine optimization skill. When you conduct keyword research, you find relevant keywords that individuals are searching for within the search engines. These keywords can then be strategically used within your blog posts to drive targeted search engine traffic to your site. Keyword research can be extremely complicated, but certain tools make the process easier:

- Moz Keyword Explorer – This program helps strategize the best optimization for your website. Plans start as low as $59 per month.

- Google AdWords Keyword Planner tool – This tool is free and easy to use for both new and experienced users. Sign up for an AdWords account before beginning your search.

- Google Trends – This is a great way to see what the latest trending stories are.

- Wordtracker's Free Keyword tool – The basic keyword search is free. However, if you wish, you can upgrade to any of their plans to receive the top trending keyword results. Plans start as low as $27 per month.

Step 5: Create Unique Content

At a loss as to what to include in your first post? You can share personal stories, tips, recipes—whatever suits your fancy. With each post, you are building a relationship with your reader so make the posts informative and helpful. Include information that they won't find anywhere else.

Step 6: Promote Your Site on Places like Facebook and Twitter

Whenever you publish a new blog post, share it with your followers on any social media channels you visit and enjoy. Encourage your followers to share with their friends. Here are some additional tips:

- ➢ Make attention-grabbing headlines.
- ➢ Use an image relevant to the headline.

➤ Make a short, compelling description of what they will find when they click on your post.

Step 7: Monetize Your Blog

Once you've started to build a solid audience for your blog, it's time to monetize it. There are different ways to monetize, depending on what type of content you have on your site.

Google AdSense

When you're just starting out, Google AdSense can be a great way to kick off your advertising and moneymaking efforts for your site. With AdSense, you are given a code for the size of the ad you'd like to place on your site, and then Google displays relevant ads based on your content or things your site visitor has shown interest in previously. You are paid each time someone clicks on an ad on your site. Depending on how much traffic you get and how likely your visitors are to click, that could equal a sizable amount of cash fairly quickly. At the very least, it will bring you a small amount of income you can contribute toward costs of maintaining or initializing the site while it gets up and running.

Site Sponsors

Another way to make money with a blog is via site sponsors or people who purchase ads or reviews on your site directly. In order to get companies to buy ads, your site needs to be up and running for a bit of time. You'll need a substantial amount of traffic. Any prospective advertisers will want to see verifiable site data, including how many unique visitors you have each month, how many pages are viewed on your site each month, and how long each site visitor tends to stick around when they do visit.

When your site builds up a huge following, however, you can start selling ads for big bucks. Some larger companies will pay thousands of dollars per month for prime placement on a popular site.

Selling Products

Another great way to earn income on your site is to sell affiliate products. As an affiliate, you'll promote specific goods and services and earn a commission each time someone buys from your site. For instance, you might write a post about a great book you read (like this one—hint, hint) and use an affiliate link from Amazon to link to the book.

Having a blog can be a fun way to meet new people and possibly earn a little cash on the side in the process.

Website: http://bit.ly/2aP4C5o/

9. Outsourcing - Utilizing the Skills of Expert Freelancers

Earning Potential: Varies, depending on your ability to secure contracts with your freelance staff.

Time Required: Varies, depending on the amount of freelancers you hire and the number of projects you outsource.

You've probably never thought of hiring freelancers as an opportunity to earn passive income. Well, it certainly can be! With this passive income idea, you will hire other freelancers (writers, editors, graphic designers, programmers, administrative assistants, and everyone in between). Although you will market the services and will ultimately oversee your workers, this business can typically run itself—assuming, of course, that you hire the right people to run your freelance enterprise.

You'll need people on your team who are not only highly competent but trustworthy and honest, contractors who will treat your clients with respect and make you both a ton of money. What you don't want are people who promise the moon, and deliver nothing but empty promises and excuses after excuses.

Some sites to find quality workers are Upwork, Fancy Hands, Time etc Limited, and Freelancer. These sites make finding the type of freelancer you need for your projects very simple. You'll select the category that you need help in—for example, writing, graphic design, or coding, etc. Once you select the category you need, each site will provide you with a list of qualified freelancers who fit your needs. You then review the freelancers' past feedback, and "interview" or screen the applicants with a test assignment to determine the best fit for you.

When you're managing a team of freelancers, keep these tips in mind:

1. **Hire freelancers slowly but fire quickly.** Take your time when hiring freelancers and don't be afraid to let someone go if they can't exceed client expectations. Be crystal clear about payment structures, deadlines, and quality of work expected. If you will be dealing with sensitive client information, always have freelancers sign a nondisclosure agreement. Be leery of contractors who consistently fail to meet deadlines. Although a couple excuses are acceptable as situations come up. However, if there is a steady pattern of late or shoddy work, broken promises, unmet expectations, and personal issues, it is time to let that freelancer go, no matter how much you like them as a person.

2. **Know your teams' strengths and weaknesses.** Always be aware of your teams' talents and be willing to improve any skills that they may be lacking. For instance, if you'd like to implement a new project management software program, provide training to get everyone up to speed on how to use it.

3. **Market their skills effectively.** You must always be on the lookout for your next team project. Either you, or someone you hire, should be searching for opportunities to keep your staff gainfully employed at all times. A small portion of your time should be spent on daily marketing, including social media marketing. Of course there will be lapses in the number of projects you obtain; however, if you steadily market, you will not notice any major dips in income for you or your staff.

4. **Charge clients appropriately.** Pay your workers an adequate rate but charge your client enough to make it worth your time. For instance, factor in expenses, taxes, contractor rates, needed profits, etc., when setting your rates. The worst thing you can do is not charge enough so you can't retain quality freelancers.

5. **Be clear about expectations.** Always be clear about what you expect from your freelancers. Company guidelines help clarify what you're looking for.

6. **Automate any processes.** To minimize your involvement with the company's freelancers, always look for ways to automate the process. For instance, if you require all articles to be fact-checked and well-written and meet specific requirements, ask your freelance writers to pass on their completed work to your editor, who will then approve and pass it on to the client, all the while keeping you out of the loop. Programs like FreshDesk make this process very easy. FreshDesk is a customizable automation program that you can completely tailor to the needs of your team. It will help you automate the workflow for each project and each client. FreshDesk allows you to set up "canned responses" and track time worked by each freelancer.

7. **Consider your title.** You may want to refrain from referring to yourself as a freelancer or freelance writer and instead call yourself a consultant or team manager. Consultants can typically charge much higher fees for their services, which will allow you to boost your profit margin.

In conclusion, using the talents of other freelancers is a great way to make passive income. Follow the above-mentioned tips to ensure that you hire the right people and maximize the skills of your team so you consistently exceed your clients' high expectations.

Websites: FreshDesk (https://freshdesk.com/)

and Upwork (http://www.upwork.com/)

10. Affiliate and Network Marketing

If you have a website, blog, or social media account with a significant following, then affiliate and network marketing can be an excellent way for you to pick up some passive income without requiring very much work. We talked a little about affiliate marketing in the last section but will now go into more detail about this very lucrative passive income stream.

Affiliate marketing works through a process where businesses reward affiliates for each customer or visitor converted through the affiliates' efforts. If you have a website or a blog, you can sign up to one or more affiliate marketing programs to drive visitors to these businesses and generate revenue for yourself.

The way this typically works is through a hyperlink. While the link will look just like any other to someone who clicks on it, the site you're directing them to, via said link, will mark that the visitor came from you. In some instances, you can even cloak the link so it doesn't show your extremely long referral code when someone puts their cursor over the hyperlink. There are many benefits of this: the shorter links are easier to manage and update, look cleaner, prevent your links from getting hijacked by hackers, etc. Check out Wordpress plug-ins, like Affiliate Link Cloaking, Pretty Link Lite, and Simple URLs.

For instance, Amazon has an affiliate program that allows people to insert a small code into a hyperlink when they recommend individual items from the site. When someone clicks on that item and buys it, Amazon gives the person who made the recommendation a small percentage of the sale. However, your affiliate link may be www.whateveryoursiteis.com/amazon/nameofproduct/12345—but, when you cloak it, you can make it www.whateveryoursiteis.com/amazon. Looks much better, right?

While you're not going to get rich off just a few affiliate items, if you continuously expose your followers to the links included in your blog posts and website materials, then you can grow your affiliate earnings into something substantial.

Other affiliate programs provide ad copy and banners, and all you do is promote this on your web property. It's very easy to get started. There are no fees to sign up, and you can be an affiliate marketer no matter where you live in the world. Something like a banner can be placed at the top of your site, similar to an AdSense ad, but then used to generate significantly more income.

Typically you can make $50–$100 daily once you get the hang of this business. Some affiliate marketing networks where you can get started are: Amazon, eBay Partner Network, ShareASale, and Rakuten Marketing.

With each company, the way you go about affiliate marketing will be slightly different. With some, you'll pick and choose what products and services you promote on your site, while, with others, you might be assigned particular products and services that the company feels would resonate particularly well within your network.

Payments for your work vary from service to service too. Many companies will only pay you when you reach a certain threshold with the service. For instance, you might need to earn $100 before you can receive a payout. Once you do reach that threshold, then payments are typically made on some organized schedule. For instance, Amazon affiliate payouts are monthly. Payments are made for referrals that happened several months prior so you can know in advance what types of payment to expect.

Those payments can come in a variety of different forms also. For instance, you may choose to be paid electronically via PayPal or direct deposit to your bank account, or you may choose to be paid through a paper check. It will ultimately depend on the company and their payment methods for affiliates.

Websites: Amazon (http://www.amazon.com),

eBay Partner Network (www.http://bit.ly/2bovrDE),

ShareASale (https://www.shareasale.com/),

and Rakuten Marketing (http://marketing.rakuten.com/).

11. Email Marketing

Earning Potential: Varies, depending on the size of your mailing list and the popularity of the product advertised.

Time Required: One to two hours to craft the cutting-edge email.

Email marketing is actually an offshoot of affiliate marketing. With emails, you not only build strong strategic partnerships with prospects and customers but you do so with trust, sincerity, and respect. And the really good news is that you inform them about something absolutely fantastic and new that could ultimately improve the quality of their lives. Wow! Pretty amazing, right?

With this passive income method, you're a salesman with your words. You send out a hard-hitting and benefit-laden email message that entices your target audience to buy whatever product or service you're selling. Therefore, it is important to have the right offering that compels your readers to buy now. Your copy must push gently but not too hard to turn people off.

This is a fine line not to cross. People are adept at deciphering bull and will report your message as spam if you keep sending annoying emails trying to sell them a bunch of crap they don't care about or need. Therefore, you not only need a quality list of buyers but your prospective buyers must trust you and see you as an authority figure—someone they trust to not only deliver solid and usable content but to provide great advice that they can use. Then, like magic, when you tell them about an incredible offer, they not only listen but they quickly pull out their credit or debit cards and buy whatever you're offering right then and there.

If done right, you can make upward of $50 to tens of thousands of dollars with one single email blast. Here's how to make email marketing work for you.

1. Be realistic about the amount of money that can be made by email marketing. Your success will depend on:

    - Your efforts and knowledge about marketing.

- The size and quality of your email list.

- The relevance of the service or product promoted to your subscribers.

- The effectiveness of what you write to market the product or service.

2. Know your target audience and woo them with quality information before you sell them anything at all. Really get to know your targeted audience. Visit forums and websites to understand their likes and dislikes. Understand current issues that affect them and solve their problems with workable solutions (these solutions should be part of your affiliate program of course). Give them useful content that provides value and builds a stronger relationship. Respect your personal relationship with them and build rapport and trust. For instance, if your target audience is people who are considering divorce, give them a steady flow of free articles or reports about how to tell if their relationship is over, how to improve a stagnant relationship, and so on. Then you can pitch your $499 course on improving their relationship or whatever item you want to sell them.

3. Don't abuse your list. The people on your list trust you so don't bombard them with frequent messages. Instead space your emails so that you are fresh on their minds but not too fresh that you get on their nerves. In a study done on twenty-one-million email messages sent to people located around the USA, the most interesting data gained therefrom was that people responded to emails better during certain hours of the day and on certain days of the week.

First, the hours to get the highest email response are between 8:00 a.m. and 10:00 a.m., and from 8:00 p.m. onward. Almost 24% of all emails sent during these times are opened but only if the emails are sent within or around an hour of these times. Once the emails remain unopened for over twenty-four hours, chances of them getting thrown in the Trash folder is 99%. However, if a person receives too many emails from you and others, suffering from in-box clutter, chances increase that your emails will be junked.

Second, based on ten different studies on email marketing, the best day to send emails is a Tuesday. However, if you want to send emails twice a week, pick Wednesday or Thursday as your second email day. All studies show that peak activities for most people are these three days. It's probably true because of the Monday blues and then the TGIF frame of mind for many, many people!

As for the number of emails to be sent weekly, experts highly recommend sending one daily but only if you have something new to offer, like a discounted promotion or a new product launch. Otherwise, it would be best to keep it to a handful every month.

4. Only offer well-researched products from established and honest companies. Only partner with companies that have a history of paying their affiliates. For instance, I once had a site about bacterial vaginosis that offered incredible free advice to women suffering from this annoying health issue. I built my mailing list to over two thousand subscribers by delivering fresh content that actually helped them. I sent bimonthly emails to share pertinent info and to encourage them. Then I partnered with a company that sold a natural supplement to alleviate bacterial vaginosis. The company seemed legit, and the product sounded great. To be honest, I didn't delve much into its effectiveness as the commission seemed awesome. Well, the product was junk. It didn't help at all, and I never received $1 from the thousands of products I sold from my email blast. I also lost subscribers and tarnished my reputation by selling this company's junk. Lesson learned: It's not about the money. It's

about doing the right thing, and the money will come. Be careful choosing you partners (in business and otherwise)!

5. Craft your marketing emails well. Use a short but catchy title that speaks to the heart of your subscriber. Always list the benefits of your recommended products in a way that encourages readers to buy without sounding too promotional.

- ✓ Personalize your email although avoid using the names of your subscribers. Thus, use analytics to find out the specific purchases or needs of your subscribers and send them emails that address these.

- ✓ Short and sweet subject lines (less than ten words) get over 50% more attention than drawn-out teasers.

- ✓ Offer free tools, templates, contests, and other giveaways.

- ✓ Optimize your emails for mobile devices.

- ✓ Use social media by sharing content thru social media links or creating a social media landing page.

- ✓ Use aesthetically pleasing visuals and hard-hitting copy!

6. Rotate the services and products that you promote. Balance nonpromotional and helpful information with promotional messages. Always work hard to build trust in your readers and to not piss them off.

7. Evaluate your ad's effectiveness. There are several goals to aim for with email marketing:

- ➢ Click-through rate – The number of subscribers who click on a link in your email.

- ➢ Conversion rate – The percentage of your email subscribers who have clicked on a link and proceeded to act on said link, whether it be a purchase, filling out a form, accepting an offer, or subscribing.

- Bounce rate – The percentage of emails that cannot be delivered, although you must know the difference between a hard and a soft bounce. The soft bounce is usually a temporary situation, like a change of email address or a full in-box, whereas a hard bounce refers to a subscriber who has closed his email address or gave you an invalid address.

- Subscriber growth rate.

- Forwarding rate – The rate on the number of subscribers who share something on your email or forwarded your email.

- Overall ROI on email marketing.

Email marketing is called the king in Internet marketing because a well-planned campaign can generate as much as 3,800% in returns or about $38 for every $1 you spend. Many companies are automating their email marketing, but only those who have a responsive strategy have higher hopes of converting emails into sales. This means that there is a person behind the email whom a potential buyer can contact and chat with concerning a purchase or concern.

In conclusion, the passive income you achieve from a successful email blast has the potential to make you a lot of money. However, you must follow the above tips to be most successful. Offer a bonus service or product if a subscriber signs up or buys something through your link.

12. Designing and Selling T-Shirts

Earning Potential: Varies, depending on the popularity of your T-shirt designs and pricing, or T-shirts sold to customers.

Time Required: Varies, depending on the intricate nature of your design.

Are you creative? Do you have some graphic design skills? Have you ever created any T-shirts? Would you enjoy creating T-shirts for others? If you answered yes to any of these questions, you should create T-shirts for passive income. Yes, it is true. People will pay you cold hard cash for your designs. Not only is this passive income stream fun but it enables you to create unique designs that people from all over the world will love and purchase.

Here are a few online marketplaces and T-shirt companies that will partner with you in exchange for a commission.

Zazzle

Zazzle provides two ways of earning money, including designing T-shirts or becoming an associate. As a designer, you will utilize your unique talents to creatively design T-shirts for consumers, while Zazzle completes the remainder of the work on your behalf. To get started, create a Zazzle account, open a free Zazzle store, create and post the design, and set up your royalty amount. In return, Zazzle will handle the printing, shipping, and customer service aspects for you. You determine your earnings utilizing Zazzle's Name Your Royalty program. Through this program, you will choose a royalty rate ranging from 5%–99%. Zazzle increases the price of the product to ensure you earn the requested royalty percentage.

If you'd rather earn money as an associate for Zazzle, follow three simple steps to begin the free process. First, create a Zazzle account. After that, you will receive a referral ID. Post your unique referral link to your blog, website, or social media account to start earning money. Every time a visitor clicks on your unique link and completes a purchase from Zazzle's website, you will earn a 15% referral fee.

Spreadshirt

In addition to Zazzle, Spreadshirt is a custom printing and T-shirt company that encourages you to design personalized and unique T-shirts to make cash. Like Zazzle, they offer two selling options. You can either upload and sell your designs to Spreadshirt via their marketplace or create an online store where you market your designs to your targeted audience. Either way, you'll create a Spreadshirt account and set your own commission rate. If you're unsure about how much to charge, the website features an estimation calculator that allows you to estimate your earnings to maximize profits before selling your design at a specific price. If you prefer to create an online store, you can customize your store's layout and even embed your online store on your site or blog. This enables you to sell your T-shirts directly from your site. Spreadshirt doesn't currently charge a fee to use this service.

Teespring

Another T-shirt company that offers a fun and easy way for designers to make some extra cash is Teespring. With their service, you can upload your own custom design, using images and text, and then sell that design to customers. The best part is that Teespring handles the actual selling, printing, and shipping of your shirt, so all you do is design it. The more shirts you sell, the more money you make. That means, it's often worth it to promote your work within your network or through something like targeted ads on social media.

Websites: Zazzle (http://www.zazzle.com/),

Spreadshirt, (https://www.spreadshirt.com/)

and Teespring (https://teespring.com/

13. Selling Your Photos

Earning Potential: Varies, depending on the popularity of the photos and the price or the number of photos sold to individuals.

Time Required: Varies, depending on the number of photos you take.

Looking to make some extra cash? Well, selling photography could be the way to go. You may already have a large collection of photos on your computer and phone, and you could sell these and earn some cash. Shutterstock.com and iStockphoto.com are just two websites that allow photographers to sell their photos to buyers for a profit. While initially sellers earn lower percentages, such as 15%, this number can increase based on granting exclusivity to one website. It's all about quantity—if you're earning an average of $1 per photo, your chances of making more money increases as your portfolio gets bigger.

These sites allow amateurs and hobbyists with a passion for photography to start selling their photos online. Make sure to submit your photos to more than one site. There are different customer bases for each site, and there is no reason for you to limit yourself to just one customer base. You can begin uploading your photos to your portfolio as soon as you are accepted as a contributor. Make a goal of how many photos you want to upload weekly. Consider what your photos will be used for and be sure not to have any recognizable brands in your photos. If this happens, you will be required to get a property release signed before you will be allowed to sell the photo. Also don't capture unknown people in your photo or you may violate their Right of Publicity statute in the state where they reside.

You can also help improve the chances of selling your images by using the right keywords. Think of how someone may look up your photo using a search engine and go from there. The more photos you submit, the more money you can make. Don't get discouraged if your photo is rejected. While a photo may be rejected by one or two sites, it may be accepted by five. Learn from the rejections. Take criticism and use it to your advantage to take better photos.

One way to avoid having photos rejected is to check the sharpness of the picture. Resizing an image will increase sharpness in the photo. Check your photos for noise; this is any pixilated or grainy area. The best way to keep noise out of your photos is to set your digital SLR to the lowest ISO. Resizing the photo can also help reduce any noise that may appear in a larger photo. When submitting a picture of a flower or insect, be sure to use the scientific name in the keywords. Leave room for publishers to add text to the photos, and don't upload too many photos or the same theme. Also be sure to check the list of "wants" and "don't wants" if the site has them before submitting your photos.

Here is a list of established websites that pay you for your high-quality photos:

iStock Photo – **Photo-Selling Site #1**

iStock Photo allows photographers to sell stocks images and receive a flat rate for each sale. If you only uploaded your images to iStock and no other stock photography sites, then you can earn a minimum of $0.34 for each download. If you work with other sites, then the minimum is slightly lower, $0.28. In order to reach exclusive status, your photos must also have been downloaded a minimum of 250 times on the site with a minimum 50% approval rating, or have been downloaded 500 times in general.

Payments are made in US dollars and are only transferred to your account once your earnings have exceeded $100. Interested photographers first become iStock members and should read the training manual for contributors. Afterward you'll be prompted to upload a few sample images to show off your work and prove it is iStock-worthy. The iStock staff members review those photos, and, if they like what they see, they'll approve you as a contributor.

Shutterstock – **Photo-Selling Site #2**

Shutterstock is a popular site for both stock photographs and buyers. The site typically sells images as part of a subscription package that initially starts out by paying contributors $0.25 each time one of their images is downloaded. As your photos are downloaded more, you receive larger amounts of money. When you sell $500 worth of photos, for instance, your rate rises to $0.33 per image. When you reach $3,000, the rate rises to $0.36, and when you sell $10,000 worth of images, your rate grows to $0.38 per image.

Rates are a bit higher when your images are sold to corporate clients. For those, earnings start at 20% of the sale price and increase to 25%, 28%, and 30% when you reach those same earnings thresholds as mentioned above. The rates for individually downloaded images are the same. You can sign up to be a contributor on the site and must provide some personal information (including a photo of your driver's license) before you can start contributing.

Fotolia – Photo-Selling Site #3

Fotolia has been a popular stock-photography site for over ten years and currently boasts a catalog of over fifty-nine million images. The company is now part of the Adobe family, which means images you upload can be sold through Adobe's stock marketplace as well as through fotolia.com. Every image you upload to the site must be at least 2400x1600 pixels. Photographers can earn between 31%–61% per image, with more money available for images and photographers who are exclusive to the site, not uploaded elsewhere. Since the service is owned by Adobe, photographers who upload their images to Fotolia can also sell them directly from within Photoshop CC, Illustrator CC, and several other apps.

Websites: iStock Photo (http://www.istockphoto.com/),

Shutterstock (http://www.shutterstock.com/),

and Fotolia (https://us.fotolia.com/).

14. Starting Your Own YouTube Channel

Earning Potential: Varies, depending on how many videos and subscribers you have.

Time Required: One to two hours to set up a customized YouTube channel; and one to two hours to make and edit a video, and upload it to your channel.

YouTube was created by Steve Chen, Chad Hurley, and Jawed Karim in February of 2005. Google purchased YouTube in November of 2006 for $1.65 billion, and it is now operated as one of Goggle's subsidiaries. The site allows users to view, share, rate, comment, and upload videos. Most of the content on the site is uploaded by individuals; however, some media corporations—such as BBC, CBS, Vevo, and Hulu—offer videos on YouTube.

Although this opportunity is semipassive, you must create fresh videos that people want to view, and then individuals must watch the videos and click on the ads to earn revenue. However, once those videos are up, and you have a steady flow of viewers, your income can grow.

Uploaded videos should be fifteen minutes or less. After a user has a good track record with complying with the company's guidelines, the user may be given the ability to upload videos for as long as twelve hours.

To start earning money on YouTube, set up and build your YouTube channel. Add keywords to help people find your videos. Be sure that your keywords are relevant to the content on your channel. Make your username something that people can remember easily.

Your uploaded content should be high quality and unique. This includes uploading videos regularly and making each video better than the last one. Review feedback and see what viewers liked or disliked about your videos and then strive to make them better than before. By uploading files on a regular basis, you will build your brand and grow your following. Users are more likely to subscribe to your channel if you add content on a regular basis. YouTubers who post daily are more likely to have more followers than someone who posts once a year.

Make eye-catching descriptions for your videos to grab people's attention when they search for relevant keywords. As more people subscribe, a greater number should be watching your videos. Therefore, you can make more money as they click your ads. The click revenue may seem tiny, but it will certainly add up over time.

Before you can start earning money on your videos, you should set up a Google AdSense account. It is free, and you must be eighteen years of age or older to create your account. Input your tax and mailing information upon sign-up. Once you're approved, your Google AdSense account will be linked to your YouTube account and used to generate revenue. Once you reach the $100 threshold, you will receive payments from Google. Keep in mind that you must also enable monetization in your YouTube's account settings.

You will only make money per ad that is clicked, but it adds up over time. A great way to keep track of how well you are doing is to check your analytics. In this menu, you can see the number of video views, demographics, ad performance, and estimated earnings. You can always change the content of your videos to help attract more subscribers.

Since YouTube is performance-based, you must get more subscribers. Share your videos on your blog, social media, and even on your off-line marketing efforts. The more people who see your videos, the more subscribers you may get. And, the more subscribers you get, the more money you make.

Website: http://www.youtube.com

15. Crowdfunding

Earning Potential: Unlimited, depending on amount you invest.

Time Required: 2-3 hours to research opportunities and 30 minutes a month to reevaluate portfolio.

Crowdfunding is a process in which individuals pool their resources to support a cause or a business venture. This process enables all types of businesses to compete globally, and to gain profits for themselves and their investors. In the past, this type of venture was only available to investors with very deep pockets. However, through the Internet, individuals with modest start-up capital can profit from this venture.

According to the July 2015 GEM (Global Entrepreneurship Monitor) Global Report, approximately one hundred million start-ups are launched every year. In the United States, an estimated $1,500 is invested by someone in a start-up every second. Of course, of the one hundred million new businesses, a large majority do not succeed, which means choosing the right start-up to invest in is crucial to earning through passive income. It's not that these entrepreneurs don't have a good idea. They often have a great idea but have limited capital to implement this idea. They may not have the funds to market, build a brand, gain customers for their product or service offering, or otherwise inform their target audience about their incredible product or service. As such, they fail fast.

Enter crowdfunding—the answer to every cash-strapped entrepreneur. Crowdfunding allows everyday individuals to invest in businesses that they believe in. Businesses that have incredible potential to succeed. In return, the investor helps a company succeed and gets paid for the privilege of doing so. The interest they receive is far greater than any interest received from a bank investment. For instance, when you invest your money in the bank, whether it be in a special savings account, a fund management portfolio, or a fixed deposit, it will give you a little ROI—and truly it is *a little* (1%) compared to what you can make with a crowdfunded investment, which yields 6% and higher.

If you're interested in crowdfunding, you can get started with a mere $25. Here are two opportunities you can check out:

16. Peer-to-Peer Lending

Earning Potential: Unlimited, but you'll typically earn about 5%–10% on your initial investment (not including any defaults).

Time Required: Two or more hours of research choosing suitable companies to invest in, then earning passive income.

Kickstarter and Kickfurther are public benefit corporations that allow crowdfunding opportunities. Kickstarter is very similar to Kickfurther. Many of the businesses that post on Kickfurther actually received their initial funding for their products through Kickstarter. The easiest way to understand both of these is to discuss them one at a time.

Kickstarter

Each project listed on Kickstarter is crafted and created by the person/team behind the project. The creator of the project sets a funding or pledging goal to complete their project. The creator is completely responsible for their project; in no way does Kickstarter claim any ownership of the projects. Kickstarter is not involved in any way. They do not investigate if the creator of the project has the ability to complete their projects before they are listed on the site.

There is no guarantee that the people who make the posts will deliver or use the funds to implement the project. It is also not guaranteed that the completed project will meet the investors'/supporters' expectations. Usually there is no monetary return on the projects. Instead the investors/supporters are offered rewards such as receiving the product after it is finished. The creators maintain ownership of their work.

The investors/supporters do not pay their pledge until the project reaches its funding goal. As there is no guarantee that the project will actually be finished, the investors/supporters are advised to use their best judgment before deciding to pledge money toward a project. If the project leader does not deliver on their promises, they could be held liable for legal damages.

Kickfurther

Kickfurther is a little different. It is focused on inventory crowdfunding for small businesses. The businesses who desire funding to buy inventory seek Kickfurther investors for assistance. Not all businesses that require assistance are accepted. Each business must fill out an application and be accepted by Kickfurther before they can post any offers for investors. They are chosen by a proprietary social-credibility algorithm.

Businesses basically ask investors to purchase their inventory in exchange for a consignment rate. Once the funding goal is achieved, Kickfurther purchases the inventory and hands it over to the business, which then sells the inventory to its targeted audience. Afterward the investors are given a percentage back, based on the inventory sold.

Investors should carefully scrutinize the offer, including the terms, interest rate, how long it will take to receive profits, and then decide if they want to invest. Once the offer reaches its funding goal, the inventory is purchased for the company. Once that inventory sells, you should see a return on your investment by earning a profit from its sale.

The minimum investment is determined by the offer and the individuals investing. Currently the minimum investment is $20, and the maximum is set at 5% of a co-op's total. This limit is only for the initial twenty-four hours, and then there is no minimum investment. Once an investor chooses an offer, they make a payment; and, once the offer is fully funded, Kickfurther purchases the inventory for the company requesting the funds.

The investor is not lending money to these businesses but buying a portion of the inventory. The business then sells the inventory on consignment, meaning the investor never sees the inventory. If all goes well, the investor receives scheduled payouts that include the cost paid toward the inventory and any profit, which can range from 6% and up.

If for some reason the business can't sell the inventory within the promised time frame, the investors can vote to either give the company additional time to sell the goods and suggest different marketing strategies or discounts. The investors can also cancel the consignment contract. If the contract is canceled, the company is required to return the inventory to Kickfurther, who will then liquidate it via a third party on behalf of its members.

If the inventory is sold, but the business does not pay the investors, then the business is committing fraud, and the amount of money owed to the investors begins to earn interest, and the business can be taken to court to recoup investors' funds.

Anyone who invests money into a project on Kickstarter or to purchase inventory on Kickfurther is at risk, possibly losing either money or the chance to make a profit. This risk is small but still exists. There are ways to protect yourself before you invest.

If the creator or business is making promises that seem too good to be true, take a step back and assess the offer before deciding to invest. Take the time to research the people behind the project or business to make sure what is being promised is really happening. Don't be quick to fund or invest in a project or business just because it sounds cool. Do not invest money in a project or business if you are not prepared to take a loss.

There is a risk associated with any kind of monetary investing. Check to see if the creator or business has had successful projects before. Even if the creator of the business has had previous success, there is still a risk. Be cautious when funding or investing in a project or product for a technological device. Kickstarter requires that these types of projects have prototypes, and they must be physical prototypes, not digital.

Let's face it. In this day and age, scams are everywhere. Here are some red flags to look for before you invest.

Make sure to do a quick Google search of the creator and the business. If they do not have a presence on any major social media sites or are not found within any Google searches, ask questions. Watch for social media accounts with fake followers. Most of the time, if a follower is fake, their profiles have little or no activity. Sadly it is very easy for people to buy fake followers. Find out if the creator/business has had any prior success in their business or past projects. Make sure to check out the company backing the project or business. Look for things such as a physical address and whether it can be verified. Look for previous accomplishments, and profiles of their team members and managers.

Watch for changes to the location of the project or business. If the location changes, do not hesitate to ask for an address to verify its existence. Changing locations makes it harder to find someone, should they not deliver on their promise. Also be on the lookout for significant changes in the amount of money being invested. If the amount changes drastically at the beginning or near the end, this is a good indication that these investments could be coming from fake accounts to initiate funding or investing in their project or business.

Always ask questions. If the person or business is vague or sends confusing information, be cautious about investing. If a project or business is a legitimate investment opportunity, there should be no reason to talk in circles about it.

Websites: Kickfurther (http://www.https://kickfurther.com/)

and Kickstarter (https://www.kickstarter.com/)

17. High-Interest Banking 101: Alternatives to Banks

(Prepaid Debit Cards with Savings Accounts)

Earning Potential: Unlimited, depending on amount you invest.

Time Required: 2-3 hours to research opportunities and 30 minutes a month to reevaluate portfolio.

Although banks are generally a more lucrative option than placing your money under your mattress, banks don't always pay the best interest rate. With this in mind, investors (especially those who understand the value of passive income) often look for more lucrative methods to earn money, and prepaid debit card companies are catering to this demand.

Companies like NetSpend, Mango, Northpointe, and Consumers Credit Union have better-than-average interest rates if you invest your money with them. However, if you decide to go this route, first make sure that the company you choose meets these requirements:

- Any savings held in the company are FDIC-insured.
- Withdrawal rates and other fees are reasonable.
- Monthly charges and limits are reasonable.

Mango

Earning Potential: About $394 per year for every $5,000 invested.

Mango is a company that offers a $3-a-month prepaid debit card that is safe and convenient. It works by attaching itself to a Mango savings account. After you have activated your Mango card, you can open a savings account with as little as $1. The savings account is FDIC-insured through Sunrise Banks, NA. Savings accounts have no monthly maintenance fees.

Currently Mango offers 6% APY for balances up to $5,000. Therefore, you can earn as much as $394 per annum on the first $5,000 in your account, and you'll earn 2% on any amount over $5,000. Mango reserves the right to change the interest rate on the savings account at any time.

Mango allows you to have six transfers a month, with a direct deposit of $800 and a minimum balance of $1 to qualify at the end of each month for the 6% interest. If you can't meet the minimum requirements or don't have the $500 direct deposit, don't worry; Mango will still offer you a 2% interest rate. You are also charged a $3 monthly service fee and ATM withdrawal fees of $2.

Although there is no activation fee, the monthly fees can't be waived.

Your savings account is separate from your debit card. The debit card can be used anywhere Visa is accepted—for secure online shopping and at ATM machines. When you want to transfer funds from your checking to your savings account (or vice versa), you can do so via phone, website, or mobile app. There is also the ability to ACH funds to your Mango account, as the debit card has a routing and account number; however, there is no easy way to ACH funds out of your Mango debit card account.

To withdraw funds from the linked savings account, individuals typically transfer funds to their linked debit card and charge the card until their funds are depleted. Some individuals simply close out their account and ask Mango to issue a check for the remaining balance.

Mango cards are safe, easy, and accepted everywhere. With a bank card and a savings account with Mango, you will know that your money is growing at the best rate possible.

Website: http://www.mangomoney.com

NetSpend

Earning Potential: Varies, depending on amount you save.

Time Required: 5-10 minutes a month to review account.

Like Mango, NetSpend offers prepaid cards that are FDIC-insured and are issued by federal- and state-regulated financial institutions. NetSpend also offers a separate tiered-rate savings account at 5% APY on balances up to $1,000. There is a catch: if the Average Daily Balance is $1,000 or less, the interest rate is 4.91% on the entire balance. If the Average Daily Balance is $1,000 or greater, the interest rate paid on the balance exceeding $1,000 will be 0.49%.

Fees are associated with using the prepaid cards. For instance, if you are on the Pay-As-You-Go plan, and you choose to use your card as a credit transaction, a $1 fee will be deducted from your card account balance. If you choose to use your card as a debit transaction, a $2 fee will be deducted from your card account balance. If you are on the Fee Advantage plan, there are no fees to use the card, whether credit or debit. A $2.50 fee is charged for each ATM withdrawal, in addition to the fees charged by the financial institution.

The Pay-As-You-Go plan is free, whereas the Fee Advantage plan has a plan fee of $9.95, and the NetSpend Premier plan is $5. There is a transfer fee of $4.95 for account-to-account transfers. Balance inquiries are $0.50. A check request fee is $5.95; a replacement card is $9.95, and the account maintenance fee per month is $5.95.

Also note that there is an inactivity fee after ninety days, so most people set up an automated ACH deposit every sixty days or so to avoid this fee.

Website: http://www.netspend.com

Consumers Credit Union

Earning Potential: Varies, depending on amount you save.

Time Required: 5-10 minutes a month to review bank account.

Consumers Credit Union offers a rewards checking account available to anyone, even if you don't live in the state of Illinois. There is a $5 fee to join the Consumers Cooperative Association. There are no monthly fees and no early account termination fees. However, they do a hard pull from Equifax for credit information. You can receive up to a 4.59% APY on balances of $20,000 or less.

Because this is a rewards account, certain requirements must be met within the calendar month to get the increased interest rate. Below is a list of interest rates and the associated requirements to receive them.

- 3.09% on balances of $10,000 or less and ATM refunds:
  - You must complete twelve debit purchases without using your PIN number.
  - You must complete at least one of these within the calendar month:
    - Pay one bill using online bill-pay;
    - One direct deposit; or
    - One ACH debit.
  - You must access your online banking at one time during the calendar month.
  - Enroll and receive eDocuments.
- 3.59% on balances of $20,000 or less and ATM refunds:
  - You must complete all the requirements for the 3.09% interest rate and spend at least $500 on Visa credit card purchases.
- 4.59% on balances of $20,000 or less and ATM refunds:

- You must complete all the requirements for the 3.09% interest rate and spend at least $1,000 on Visa credit card purchases.

If these requirements are not met, you will only receive 0.01% APY. All debit transactions, direct deposits, ACH debits, or bill-pay transactions must post and clear the account before the end of the calendar month.

Website: https://www.myconsumers.org/

Northpointe

Earning Potential: Varies, depending on amount you save.

Time Required: 5-10 minutes a month to review bank account.

Northpointe offers a 5% APY UlitmateAccount (checking account) for balances up to $5,000; anything over this amount gains 0.10% interest. An initial $100 deposit is required to open the account, available nationwide. They do a soft pull on your credit when you apply for the account. There is no monthly fee, and they are FDIC-insured.

Checking accounts with a balance of $5,000 or less will receive 5% APY if these requirements are met:

- You must have $100 or more in automatic withdrawals or direct deposits each month.
- You must use your debit card to make fifteen or more purchases that total more than $500.
- You must be enrolled in eStatements.

There is an early withdrawal penalty if the account is closed before 120 days, and the offer is limited to one per household. Any bonuses are treated as income, and you must pay taxes on them. If the account has no activity for twelve months, a monthly fee of $5 is assessed.

Website: http://www.northpointe.com/

18. Credit Card Rewards

Earning Potential: Varies, depending on amount purchased on a monthly basis and reward rate of card.

Time Required: Fifteen minutes to sign up for a new card and verify security questions.

When most people use credit cards, they typically use them to make it from payday to payday, to cover emergencies, or simply to purchase items that they can't/won't pay for out of pocket. Most people don't pay attention to interest rates and typically pay the minimum balance each month. Credit card companies love consumers like this because the companies make big money off such consumers.

What these consumers don't realize is that they can easily turn the tables on the credit card companies. They can obtain and use credit cards as a powerful passive income tool to gain more wealth. Here's how it works:

When you have a credit card that offers cash back, you can then charge everyday items like groceries, gas, tuition, utilities, dinners out, etc. With every swipe, you will then earn 1% or more in cashback rewards. This is easy money for simply buying stuff that you'd already buy anyway. However, to make this method work, you must always pay off your bills every single month, without exception (before the grace period ends, and, beware, as most are less than thirty days). This strategy will prevent you from paying more in interest than you earn in rewards and will ensure that you don't pay any interest or late fees that many unsavvy credit card owners pay daily.

So, if you have good credit (preferably excellent credit) and are willing to take a hit to your credit score, you can profit from this passive income opportunity. Just remember that cashback credit cards are harder to get approved for and often have a higher interest rate than noncashback reward credit cards.

Always check www.doctorofcredit.com and offers from card issuers for up-to-date interest rates, reward terms, etc. Whenever you apply, carefully read any fine print and be aware that applying for credit cards (at banks and credit unions) is typically a hard pull on your credit and can negatively affect your credit rating. In some instances, you can apply for one to two cards with same issuer, and only one hard pull will be counted. But this depends on the individual issuer.

Here are some of my favorite credit card reward cards:

Fidelity Rewards Visa Signature Credit Card

You must be at least eighteen years old to apply for the Fidelity Rewards Visa Signature Card. You will earn two points for every $1 spent on your credit card. You can choose to have your points converted to cash on a monthly basis, or you can choose to redeem them at a time of your choosing. You must have at least five thousand points to redeem them for cash. There are no caps on the amount of points you can earn, and they do not expire. The interest rate for this card is 14.24%.

Chase Sapphire Preferred Card

The Chase Sapphire Preferred card gives you fifty thousand bonus points after you spend $4,000 within the first three months of opening the card. This is equivalent to $500 or up to $625 in Travel Rewards that are transferrable to their travel partners (United, Marriott, Hyatt Regency, British Airways, IHG, and more). You can earn two times the points for dining at restaurants and traveling. If you add another authorized user, and they make a purchase within three months, you will earn a five-thousand-point bonus. Chase offers no annual fee for the first year and then $95 thereafter. The current interest rate ranges from 16.24%–23.24% variable interest, depending on your creditworthiness.

Chase Freedom Unlimited

Chase Freedom Unlimited offers an unlimited 1.5% cashback reward on every purchase. This cashback reward is automatic. They are currently offering a $150 bonus after you have spent $500 within the first three months of opening the card. The interest rate is 0% for the first fifteen months of the account for purchases and balance transfers. After the fifteen months, the card's interest rate will be a 14.24%–23.24% variable rate and offers a 5% balance transfer fee based on your creditworthiness. The cash rewards do not expire, and you can request them at any time. There is no annual fee charged on this card.

Blue Cash Preferred Card from American Express

The Blue Cash Preferred card offers you a chance to earn $150 in rewards as an initial sign-up bonus. You must spend at least $1,000 of qualifying purchases on a new card account in the first three months to receive the statement credit. You can also earn 6% cash back at US supermarkets (up to the first $6,000 per year), 3% cash back at gas stations and select department stores, and 1% on other purchases. There is a 0% APR on purchases and balance transfers for the first twelve months, and then it rises to 13.24%–23.24%, depending on your credit. The $95 annual fee is not waivable within the first year.

BankAmericard Cash Rewards Credit Card

BankAmericard Cash Rewards Credit Card offers 0% interest for the first twelve months or twelve billing cycles on purchases. Balance transfers have a 0% transfer fee if made within the first sixty days of opening the card account. After the sixty-day period, there will be a fee of 3% for balance transfers, and the interest rate on the card goes up to 13.24%–23.24%. If you redeem your cash and have it placed into a Bank of America checking or savings account, you will earn a 10% customer bonus. This card offers a $100 sign-up bonus and 3% cash back on gasoline, 2% at grocery stores, and 1% cash back on everything else. Bank of America charges no annual fee for this card.

Barclay Rewards MasterCard

Barclaycard Rewards MasterCard has no annual fee and no limit to the number of points you can earn or redeem. They offer two times the number of points on grocery store purchases, gas, and utilities; and one time the points on all other purchases. Your points can be redeemed and deposited into a US checking or savings account, gift cards, or statement credits, and they don't expire. Every one thousand points is equal to $10. Barclaycard Rewards also give you free access to a FICO credit score to help you keep track of your credit rating. Fraud liability is free for this card, and you are not responsible for any unauthorized charges that you report to them. The variable interest rate is currently 25.24% for cash advances, purchases, and balance transfers.

Recap

As you can see, there are many options to earn passive income with reward cards. Just remember to pay off your bill before the grace period ends to avoid any fees and to truly reap the benefits of this incredible passive income idea.

Websites: American Express Preferred (http://amex.co/2aNpOct),

Fidelity Rewards (http://bit.ly/2b47jTE),

Chase Freedom Unlimited (https://creditcards.chase.com),

Barclay Rewards (http://bit.ly/2bnUAdz),

Bank Americard Cash Rewards (http://www.bankofamerica.com)

Advanced Skills Required

Designing Web Templates, Licensing Music, Creating an App,

Renting Properties, Investing Online

($500+ Income Club)

19. Selling Web Design Templates

Earning Potential: Varies, depending on the amount of templates sold.

Time Required: Depends on your skill level.

Making money selling web design templates can be very profitable, but it takes some work to make it happen. Some web designers are making anywhere from $500–$30,000 per month by selling their web design templates. Individuals are willing to pay $15–$100+ for precoded, predesigned templates they can use, royalty free, instead of paying a web designer to do it for them.

To get started, you must figure out what you're good at designing. Is it WordPress themes or plug-ins, HTML/CSS templates, PSD design files, or Magento themes? Choose one platform that you can master. Do not spread yourself too thin in the beginning. Allow people to get to know you and your design style so that you have a higher chance of success.

Decide how much of the work you are willing to do on your own. If you can do everything from the design, coding, and so on, great! If not, you may want to consider joining others who can help you develop your template. You can find suitable partners on Upwork or other freelance sites.

Just remember that the more work you do yourself means the more control you will have over how much money stays in your pocket. Having a partner will take a cut from your profits, but it is better than not selling any templates because you do not possess the skills needed to complete them. When people purchase your template, they will expect it to be top-notch. Keep on top of the latest coding trends and ensure the templates are bug-free.

Any style code, scripts, or markups included with your product should be easy to read and operate. Include as much documentation as you can in a ReadMe file to help buyers get the most from your product. Make sure to avoid support disasters by making it easy for people to use your code.

People buy web design templates to save time spent coding and designing themselves. Take the time to test your template, using it as the buyer would. Ask others to review and comment on it before making it available for purchase. Test out the template on every browser.

After you have completed all the designing, coding, and testing, figure out where you will sell your web design. A lot of great websites are out there that will do a lot of the work for you, such as support, marketing, payment processing, etc. However, they will also cut into your profits. Consider this when choosing a site to list your template on.

Here are some established sites where you can sell your web design templates to make passive income.

ThemeForest

ThemeForest is a site that allows you to sell WordPress themes, Joomla templates, Photoshop templates, and HTML templates. Your profit for selling your themes on this site will vary. If you sell exclusive themes on their site, you will receive between 35% and 50% of every sale. If you do not sell exclusive themes on their site, you will earn 25% of every sale. You must first complete a tutorial and a quiz before you can list your templates.

Templamatic

Templamatic requires that the templates are cross-browser compatible, with no copyright issues. You will earn 65% of all sales. This site is free to join and allows you to set your own prices. This site accepts Drupal, Joomla, and WordPress templates.

buystockdesign.com

The buystockdesign site allows WordPress and Joomla templates to be uploaded. Here you will make between 50% and 75% of every sale. Prices for templates usually start at $5 and go up to $25. You must have a $50 balance from sales before you can cash-out.

Recap

Selling website templates is a great way to make passive income. Once you do the initial work to bring your template to market, you can consistently make passive income each and every time it is sold.

Websites: Upwork (http://upwork.com/),

Templamatic http://www.templamatic.com/),

Theme Forest, (https://themeforest.net/)

Buystockdesign (http://www.buystockdesign.com)

20. Music Licensing

Earning Potential: Varies, depending on how many people purchase a license to your music.

Time Required: Varies, depending on how fast you can create a song.

Everyone loves a good heartfelt song, one that touches the heartstrings or makes you want to get out of your chair and dance, dance, dance. If you can sing or create songs that make others want to sing and/or dance, you should consider licensing your music as a passive income opportunity.

Music licensing ensures that the owner of the musical work is compensated for the use of their work. The person who buys the license has limited rights to use the musical work without having to sign separate agreements. To make this work, you must have a library of marketable songs or at least one.

Once you have the copyrights in place for your musical work (via www.USPTO.gov), you can choose to sell the rights to your song. You can also prevent anyone from using the lyrics (even within books), music, or performing the song without permission. You own the whole song and can choose how to license it.

Radio stations, restaurants, someone making a commercial, or anyone wanting to use your musical work must purchase rights to do so. Depending on how the musical work will be used, it can cost as much as $2,000–$500,000 to obtain the rights to use it.

As an example, the song "Happy Birthday to You" was copyrighted in 1934 and still brings in approximately $2 million per year in licensing fees. As you can see, it is important to copyright your musical work.

The website License Quote (LQ) makes it easy to manage and license your music. They are not a publisher or stock music owner. Instead they are a private label solution that helps independent musicians and publishers publish, organize, and license their music directly from their own website (or yours if you choose to link to their site from yours or embed your music store on your site).

This service enables you to keep 100% of the revenue made from the licensing of your music, and they offer a no-risk free plan to get you started. The free plan is limited to fifteen tracks and MP3 file hosting or linking. There are also subscription plans that give you full control over the offerings and pricing that start at $10 per month or $100 per year. In contrast, the LQ Manager plan includes up to 250 tracks, a fully integrated catalog, and a preview player tracker. This plan accepts MP3s, WAV, and AIF files via hosting or linking.

Here is an example of some of the licensing prices you may set:

- Audio projects, $260
- Games and software, $750
- Products and toys, $150
- Radio ad, $175
- Slide show or PowerPoint, $100
- Telephone or on-hold music, $12
- TV advertising, $122
- Composition and sound recordings, $75
- Film sync license, $210
- Public space, such as, retail spaces, trade shows, and restaurants, $120
- Sampling, remixes, covers, and derivative works, $90
- Software, all platforms, any use, $150
- Video (music videos, CD-ROM, or DVD), $130
- Corporate, theater, and competition, $50
- Internet-web flash, $55
- Music compilations, $150

- Mechanical royalty (up to five minutes), $0.091 per copy

- Mechanical royalty (over five minutes), $0.0175 per minute, per copy.

No prices are set in stone. You can change the prices for any of the license types at any time. As the publisher you have complete control to adjust or accept the pricing for each type of license to meet your catalog's marketing needs. Buyers can choose your fixed price, or buyers can make an offer. You then have the option to negotiate prices with those who are interested in purchasing a license to use your work.

To get started with LicenseQuote, create your marketable music or get someone else to create it for you, copyright the end product with your copyright office, and register your library with your local Performance Rights Organization (PRO). (Use Google to find your local PRO.)

Your PRO negotiates nondramatic licensing agreements for producers and songwriters, and acts as a copyright collection agency. For instance, for some license types, the PRO may not deal with the buyer at all, and, for others, the PRO may send bills for additional performance royalties. It will depend on the contract and your agreement. Either way, you'll then set up your licensing store with LicenseQuote that features a clear-cut music licensing agreement (which you should have reviewed by your attorney before signing). You'll select preferred currency, choose a brand name, a list rate card or individual prices, promote your store, and make money when someone buys a license to your music.

Keep in mind that, although everything is pretty automated with LicenseQuote (once you get the system initially set up), you'll work closely with your PRO representative to oversee fund collection. You'll also cover any expenses, including payment to composers, musicians, or producers you've hired (with future royalties or upfront payments), evaluate sales, engage in additional social media and online marketing to promote your library, etc.

IMPORTANT: Licensing is complicated. I strongly recommended that you contact a licensed attorney to assist you.

Websites: CD Baby (http://www.cdbaby.com/)

and LicenseQuote (Http://www.licensequote.com)

That said, if you've got musical talent, licensing is a fun way for you to share your talents with others. Use it the right way and your creativity can surely pay out, whether you license your work to one or millions. After all, no one wants to die with their music inside them. Instead create songs and get paid passive income for them.

CD Baby

CD Baby offers hosting for independent artists for online music distribution. Some of the services include digital and physical distribution; shipping CDs, DVDs, and vinyl; warehouse storage, disc duplication, web-hosting and design, etc. This means that anyone who has not sold their work to a corporation is eligible to store and sell their music here. It is a company run by musicians for musicians.

As an independent music artist, if you sell your music through CD Baby, you will receive $6–$12 per album, and the pay is weekly. Over 360,000 different albums are currently being sold, and three million tracks are in the digital distribution catalog, with $157 million having been paid directly to the artists.

You must be at least thirteen years of age or older to sign up for an account, and a one-time $49 charge ($89 for pro) will set up your CD in the store. A $9.95 fee is charged for a single track ($34.95 for pro). CD Baby keeps $4 of every vinyl or CD sold and 9% of all digital sales.

There is a free option available. You set your selling price for downloads, and CD Baby keeps 15%. You also decide when you are paid. You will set up a pay limit, and, once your account reaches that amount, you will get paid on the following Monday, either through ACH, Payoneer, or PayPal. There is a $2 fee for paper checks and a $2.50 fee for ACH direct deposit.

21. Creating an App

Earning Potential: Varies, depending on the amount of apps sold.

Time Required: Depends on your skill level.

Just look around you. Almost everyone, from tots to seniors, knows how to work a smartphone. Individuals love apps and use them every single day! Therefore, if you're looking to join a very hot and profitable market, you should consider creating and selling an app. You don't even have to be an experienced app designer or even have deep pockets to get your dream app made. You can simply hire someone off Upwork to handle all the technical aspects while you watch the profits roll in.

Now, before you get started, you must keep a few things in mind. First and most important, you must do your market research to discover which apps are hot and which ones are not. You must read specs and reviews to determine which apps have the features that people crave. The Apple Store and the Google Play store both display top paid and free apps, information vital for anyone wanting to enter the app market. Once you've conducted your initial research, start generating ideas about potential apps you'd like to create. Really think about your app.

Ask yourself these questions:

1. Will my app have custom or modified firmware?

2. What type of app will it be? For instance, will it be a fully dynamic app, database-driven with custom functionality, basic table functionality, gaming app, or another type?

3. What is my budget for app creation?

4. Do I have any programming skills, like Objective-C, Java, PHP, Ruby, and/or C#? If not, am I willing to learn these skills?

5. Can I create the design myself? If not, you should at least sketch out your idea (including splash screens, icon, etc.) to share your vision with your programmer.

6. What is my specific budget? Keep in mind that app development ranges from $1,000 to $50,000 or more, depending on type and features.

7. Do you want an iOS or Android app?

8. What is the general design flow of the app?

9. Will you make money with your app? Will it be free, or will you charge a certain fee per download?

10. What marketing strategies will you use?

11. Will you offer in-app paid features to generate additional revenue?

Once you have answered these questions, shorten your list to your top one or two apps. Then conduct some market research. Ask friends, family, and acquaintances if they'd be interested in a few of your designs. Get feedback and review it carefully. After all, you want a winning design that is nice-looking, easy-to-navigate, and in high-demand.

Next, take the feedback you obtained from others and develop the app that seems to be most appealing to you and users. Visualize success. Think Pokemon Go, only better. If you're designing your own app, get busy. If you're working with a designer, create a design via Photoshop that is easy-to-understand and carefully organized. Interview experienced programmers and inform them about the features you are searching for in your app. The programmer you choose should be technologically savvy, easily accessible, honest, hardworking, excited about working with you, and willing to create your app to your precise specifications. Note: Always be crystal clear about expectations and have a written agreement that includes deliverables, deadlines, and payment terms.

By now, you should have a beta version of the app to evaluate. Carefully go through the debugging process and make changes before you post it live to avoid any negative feedback and customer dissatisfaction. You can hire contractors at sites like TryMyUI to test your app and provide feedback for it.

Once your app is ready to be put in the iTunes store, set up an iTunes Connect account ($99) for your other future apps too. They will then charge you 30% of all sales. Through the backend of iTunes Connect, you can monitor analytics, downloads, etc. Either way, you should get feedback on it from your beta testers.

If you're downloading to the Google Play store, you should sign up for a Google Play Developer account and pay the initial fee ($25). Once you're set up, log in to your Developer Console, select All Applications and then Add New. It will thereafter prompt you to upload your app.

After you've submitted your app to the platform of your choice, the approval process can take two to three weeks, after which your app is officially released to the market. During this time, you should be ramping up your marketing efforts. If they are working, keep at it. If they're slowing down or not gaining traction, figure out why so you can improve your app with the next version.

22. Renting Properties

Rental properties are hot. Last year the rental industry for commercial properties grew by 9%. As for apartment rentals, the average growth also increased by a whopping 4.6% in 2015 alone. And this trend doesn't seem to be slowing down.

Experts anticipate that young working adults, married folks, and couples living together without children will continue to rent apartments instead of buying a house and taking out a mortgage. In fact, the percentage of first-time house buyers has dropped significantly in the last thirty years. Apartment renting is preferred because it is more economically feasible and allows for more flexibility.

So, if you're looking for a sound passive income investment, consider buying a house, mobile home, or apartment to rent out. Assuming you make a wise initial investment, your income could grow exponentially as you raise rents every year. According to RealPage, Inc., a property management software provider, the average annual income for apartment renters today is $85,000 (for a two-income situation), so paying $1,200 in monthly rent ($14,450/year) is palatable because it only represents 17% of their income. Rent is traditionally known to grow faster than inflation and wages, and people put that cost first into their budget because they need a place to live.

So consider entering the real estate market. Here are two ideas to help you earn a profit:

Rent Out Space with Airbnb (http://www.airbnb.com)

Earning Potential: $100+ a month (varies, depending on how many properties you have available).

Time Required: Two to three hours to set up and take photos of properties, and then four or more hours a month to handle inquires, clean properties between guests, etc. Of course this can be automated with a cleaning service but will cut into your profits.

Airbnb is an online community that matches people who need a place to stay with people who are open to renting out their apartments, homes, boats, castles, etc. In essence, your listed property gets converted into a "bed and breakfast" when you aren't using it. Think of it as owning your own Hyatt Regency without actually owning a hotel. You can transform wasted space or storage space in your home into a potential source of income.

To get started, you'll list your user profile and then take photos of your property, and write a clever title and description to capture the attention of travelers. Information will include price, size of property, amenities (pool, sauna, whirlpool, and so on). Next, travelers use the Airbnb to look for properties that meet their needs and contact you if they're interested in renting yours out. Once a match is made, travelers can book the property by choosing the Book It feature. They then pay the host's requested fee and an additional 6%–12% to Airbnb as a guest service fee. Once the host confirms and the traveler pays, the full amounts (including service fees) are sent via PayPal, Google Wallet, paper checks, or credit/debit card (Visa, MasterCard, American Express, and Discover). The funds are put in escrow, and the payment is released to the host twenty-four hours after check-in.

Pros

- You'll earn extra passive income for renting out your home or apartment while providing individuals with the opportunity to stay at a nice local property.

- Hotels aren't always the best places, and, if you have a nice property listed on Airbnb, it will be in high demand because you can give travelers a richer and nicer experience.

- Oftentimes Airbnb is significantly cheaper than a hotel. So you'll help out the community of travelers by saving people money without paying outrageous amounts of money.

- If you live in a high-priced rental area, like NYC, and have a loss of income or simply want to save money, Airbnb can allow you to cut costs and make income without losing your property.

- You can accept or deny anyone without repercussions, or cancel if you have a good excuse for doing so.

Cons

- You make a profit, but you must factor in ownership costs, like mortgage, insurance, taxes, electricity, water/sewer, housecleaning service, gas for appliances or heat, cable, Internet, TV, toiletry supplies, etc.

- You must put in a bit of time answering inquiries, taking pictures of property, and making sure everything is fairly stocked.

- You will have strangers staying at your place.

- If you had month-to-month tenants, you'd have one set of people, but, with Airbnb, you'll have multiple people staying within a given month.

- You should provide clients with such items as dishwashing detergent, trash can liners, towels, shampoo, soap, toilet paper, paper towels, etc. Often people will steal these items if you keep them in a cabinet.

- Check-out is 12:00 p.m., but people leave at 1:00 p.m. Check-in is at 3:00 p.m., and people often arrive punctually, so you'll need a very reliable staff member to clean up during this extremely tight time frame between check-out and check-in.

Things to Keep in Mind

According to 26 US Code § 280A, the Internal Income Code, you must pay taxes on any rental income. This gets tricky because you must first determine if the property is "rental," a residence, or both. Your home is considered "rental" for purposes on any day it is rented for <u>fair market value</u>. This also applies to family members. If you rent your home to a family member, and they don't pay fair market value rent for any days they're staying there, it is considered rental property. If they don't pay fair market value rent or use the home as their primary residence, then such personal-use days are not taxable. It gets even more complicated. If you, your spouse, siblings, lineal descendants, or anyone you have a reciprocal arrangement with uses the house or apartment for any part of the day, it is considered being used for personal use and not taxable as rental property.

I said all that to say this, if you rent the apartment or house while you're living there, you most likely will receive a personal-use credit for the days you were there and not for the days you had someone else living there.

Example: Let's say you live in your condo for 365 days. You rent out a room for 50 days. The home will be used for personal purposes for 365 days and 50 days for rental purposes. Note: Be sure to check with your lawyer or accountant regarding this matter.

Rental Properties – Become a Landlord

Earning Potential: About $500+ a month.

Time Required: Forty hours initially; two to three hours a month to maintain property.

Income from investing in property can be a great way to earn passive income. The neighborhood you invest in matters a great deal, as this determines the amount of rent you can collect. Crime rates, proximity to downtown areas, universities and schools are all important factors. To get your foot in the property business, consider investing in mobile homes, as you'll need a lot less capital to get started than buying a traditional brick-and-mortar property. With mobile homes, expenses such as taxes and insurance are significantly less than regular homes. Average rents from mobile homes can be anywhere from $300–$500 for used homes and up to $1,000 for new ones. You'll typically pay $6,000+ for a high-quality one-to-two-bedroom mobile home, whereas you'll pay $35,000+ for a one-to-two-bedroom traditional home.

As stated above, please consider some things before purchasing a rental property. One is what kind of neighborhood the property is located in, which will influence what type tenants you will attract. For instance, it's much better to purchase the worst-looking house in the best neighborhood than the best-looking house in the worst neighborhood.

Another thing to consider is how often you will face vacancies. A property close to a university or highly populated or busy area will have fewer vacancies on a regular basis, whereas a property in a densely populated area with lots of vacant houses will have higher vacancy rates. High vacancy rates force you to charge less rent to attract new tenants or to absorb the expenses when the property is unoccupied. Fewer vacancies in popular areas allow you to charge higher rent.

Consider the cost of property taxes. Because taxes are not standard across the board, you can check with the town's assessment office to gather the tax information on the property. Even if the taxes are high, if it is a neighborhood that will attract long-term tenants, high taxes may not be such a bad thing, as you'll be in better school and park districts, with better maintenance of roads and parks, offering top-notch police facilities, libraries, and so on.

After you have found a property, always check the quality of the school system and it surroundings, because this can affect the value of the rental property. Individuals with children often want properties with good schools. A school with a poor reputation will reflect on the overall value of your rental property, should you decide to sell the property at a later time, while a school with a good reputation will command higher home prices.

Also evaluate how bad the crime is in the area. No one wants to rent in a hotspot for criminal activity. Crime statistics can be searched either in public libraries or at the police station. Look for recent activity, petty crimes, serious crimes, and vandalism rates. You can also question the police about how often their presence in needed in the neighborhood.

Bonus Tips

1. Provide your tenants with a high-quality property and you will attract quality tenants. By offering a quality property, great tenants will fight to conduct business with you. Create a written policy and stick to it.

2. Have a written policy for security deposits, rental payments, what is covered by the landlord, items the tenant is responsible for, late and unpaid rent, loud music, pets, etc., and make sure your tenants understand and abide by any conditions you set. Also have set office hours for situations (unless an emergency) so that you don't receive calls and requests at odd hours of the night. It's typically recommended to give tenants your Google number ("forwarded" to your mobile phone) so you keep your personal phone number private but are readily available to handle requests.

3. Because there is a higher chance that the renter will damage the property, rental insurance rates cost 25% more than homeowner's insurance—so keep this in mind.

4. Always evaluate the hidden costs to fix up an apartment or home before renting it out or while it is rented. For instance, you must pay advertising costs to obtain new tenants, legal fees for bad tenants, administrative fees if you hire a property management firm to oversee the rent collection process, cleaning and maintenance fees (carpet, landscaping, paint, etc.) and increased taxes (no homeowner exemption fees, as you won't reside in the home).

5. Outsource as much as you can. You're in the business to make passive income so it is best to outsource as much of your landlord duties and property management as you can. For instance, you can hire a property management company that will show the property, screen tenants, handle security deposits and rent collections, start eviction proceedings, prepare property for rent, etc. Although a do-it-yourself approach saves money, the more you can outsource, the less stressed you'll be, and the more likely you can create more income streams that will ultimately make you more money.

23. Investing Online

Now that we've delved into the easier and medium-level passive income methods, it's time to get into the more complicated methods. You've probably already heard of online investing and realize that, if you want to earn $1,000 or more a month from investment interest (leaving the principal alone), you must have $250,000 in investments earning over 5% to do so. If you don't have that much (yet), you may have simply given up on these online investments. The good news is that you don't need nearly as much to get started.

Many online stock trading exchanges and a growing number of websites understand that not everyone has that much money to invest initially. Therefore, they're willing to teach you how to invest with little to no capital. That is, certain companies are willing to invest in you by offering you funds for free to get started. The free funds are not a lot, but they should lessen any fears of losing all your money and going bankrupt with online investments.

Spark Profit

For instance, Spark Profit is one that comes to mind. According to this company's website, you do not have to have any investments to start earning. You simply make predictions about the real financial markets, and, as prices change after your prediction, your point score will go up or down based on the accuracy of your prediction. With enough points, meaning your score exceeds the weekly threshold (which is currently set at twenty thousand points), you earn money. The money may not be much (Spark Profit says top players earn $50 or more a month); however, it is something, considering that Spark Profit takes all the risk while giving players the credit for predicting accurately.

Motif

Motif is an online brokerage company built on customizable theme-based portfolios that can be traded for as low as $9.95 or $0.33 per stock. By joining Motif, investors can receive up to $150 when they start the trading process. Motif is a great brokerage firm for people just starting out. It allows you to diversify even if you don't have much to invest. You can invest in concepts like oil and biotech instead of individualized companies. The costs are relatively inexpensive and allow you to learn the market as you play around with your portfolio.

Here's a crash course about profiting from the stock market:

- Your mission with online stock trading is to buy low, sell high or sell higher than you bought (factoring in any commissions that you might have paid).

- It can be tough (if not impossible) to tell which stocks might likely increase in price and to protect yourself from fraud. Therefore, it is crucial to do your due diligence before investing in any stocks. For instance, you should evaluate their business, history, officers, and financial statements. Ideally you should research and investigate each company for at least two weeks, using the Internet and reading the current business news to figure out the latest trends before plopping down any money.

- Many financial analysts will argue that mutual funds (managed by an experienced manager) are less volatile than individual stocks, and some will recommend investing in the exchange-traded funds (ETFs) because they are simpler to understand, inexpensive, very liquid, and have good potential ROI.

- For steady income, you can invest in dividend-yielding stocks that have growth potential. Depending on the stock portfolio and the amount invested, dividends can be a substantial amount. Before you can earn any income, your first order of business is to get a brokerage account to buy and sell equities. The big brokerage houses can charge hundreds of dollars for trades, so a good idea would be to find a broker with low commission charges. For instance, OptionsHouse charges $4.95 per trade, has a good range of investment instruments, and does not require a minimum deposit. Robinhood is a zero-commission broker that allows users to choose their investments from all US-traded companies without any limitations on the stocks one can invest in.

- Two other methods of making passive income with low investments are through CD ladders and annuities:
    - CDs (certificates of deposit) are similar to bonds but have several advantages when compared to other securities, such as government bonds, including higher yields. CDs pay interest only at maturity. As they are available only through banks, they also carry FDIC insurance in the case of the bank defaulting. Laddering is a form of investing through CDs to generate a stable cash flow, where you invest in multiple CDs with different maturity dates, generating periodic income. CD laddering can be customized to provide payments monthly or annually, depending on investors' needs. To get started, get in touch with a few banks to find out your options.
    - Annuities are an investment option usually purchased from an insurance company. These investments promise to pay a certain amount of money annually for the rest of the investor's life. For instance, a 4% $20,000 annuity would mean that the investor would receive $800 for the rest of their life. Some things to keep in mind when considering an annuity are a reputable insurance company with a good bond rating.

Websites: Spark Profit (https://sparkprofit.com/),

Motif Investing (https://www.motifinvesting.com/),

Options House (https://www.optionshouse.com/)

and Robinhood (https://www.robinhood.com/)

Passive Income Streams

Conclusion

Now Make Your Passive Income Dreams Happen!

As you can see, many investment opportunities await you. Your choices are unlimited and so are your possibilities. Being open and receptive to all the methods out there, you can choose the right ones for you. Whether you choose to start small or go big, you can achieve your passive-income goals one stream at a time. Don't be afraid to dabble in various methods until you find the right combination that works for you.

When you're smarter with the money you have, you will attract even more money. Passive income streams are the key to a better and more prosperous life. With these streams, you will no longer feel like a slave to active income. You no longer must work a regular job (unless you choose to). You can go where you want and work when and if you desire. You can experience financial peace and abundance in all areas of your life. You can make money doing the things you love to do, and you can change the lives of those you care about.

Although the road may seem hard at first and will take time, don't ever give up on your dreams of financial success. Learn from your mistakes and keep pushing forward. Failure is only feedback. Steer clear of naysayers and work your plan every single day. With time, you'll make progress and be on your way to passive income success. Your future is bright and so are you! Now make it happen!

Passive Income Streams

BONUS

BEST PASSIVE INCOME RESOURCES TO CHECK OUT NOW

Passive Income Websites

ShoeMoney – Jeremy Schoemaker

ShoeMoney is the blog of Jeremy Schoemaker, sharing tips in online marketing to over thirty thousand readers. Schoemaker has made millions of dollars in this enterprise, and his blog has been named the Best Affiliate Marketing Blog. He uses his blog to share his insights with other people so that they can prosper financially.

http://www.shoemoney.com

Smart Passive Income – Pat Flynn

Smart Passive Income is an online resource that teaches readers how to run a successful online business and to use search engine optimization to bring in large amounts of passive income every year. This website offers practical, well-tested advice from Pat Flynn, who has consistently made money from the practices he now shares.

http://www.smartpassiveincome.com/

The College Investor – Robert Farrington

The College Investor is a blog with over 16,000 readers, learning to deal with their student loan debt, earning money, and building wealth. Robert Farrington has been named America's Millennial Money Expert and America's Student Loan Debt Expert.

http://thecollegeinvestor.com

Bogleheads.org

Bogleheads is an online forum, providing passive income ideas, advice on generating stable passive income, and funds to build a passive income stream. It is an online resource for investors, emphasizing an early start to building one's finances, living below your means to regularly save money, and sticking to an investment plan.

https://www.bogleheads.org/

Entrepreneurs-Journey.com – Yaro Starak

Entrepreneurs Journey is a blog for entrepreneurs interested in making over a million dollars with Yaro Starak's proven business plan. Starak has created, managed, and sold several prosperous online businesses.

https://www.entrepreneurs-journey.com

Passive Income Online Forums

BeerMoney

https://www.reddit.com/r/beermoney/

The BeerMoney forum on www.reddit.com is an incredibly active community where users share tips and ask questions about online moneymaking opportunities. The forum runs regular contests from which the winners get their referral link (to moneymakers like Swagbucks and Perk) publicly posted. There is also a curated list of the best moneymaking sites in various categories, like Easy Money and also Special Skill. This is a great place to find ways to supplement your income, whether to literally buy beer, pursue a hobby, or add to your savings account. Like on many subreddits, the huge community here is very engaged and quick to share their experiences to help you make some extra cash.

Passive Income and PassiveIncome

https://www.reddit.com/r/passive_income/

https://www.reddit.com/r/passiveincome

These subreddits devoted to passive income aren't nearly as active or as well-curated as the BeerMoney subreddit, but they still offer some quality discussions. Members share stories and ask questions about passive earning opportunities, while also pointing out great resources and recommending tools or software. These subreddits are worth looking through every once in a while, as there are some quality posts and active members. It might be easier to get a post noticed on one of these forums as well, as the communities aren't as massive as communities like BeerMoney.

Swagbucks

https://www.reddit.com/r/Swagbucks/

If you want to dive deep into how to make money with Swagbucks, this is the right place for you. While other subreddits certainly cover Swagbucks, this forum is completely devoted to it and delves into every detail. There is a great general guide to Swagbucks with a rundown of all the possible ways to earn, a bot that updates members about new codes, and the usual forum of questions and stories from community members. If you're new to Swagbucks, this is an ideal resource to learn how to maximize your efforts. It's also a great idea to check out this subreddit if you've been using Swagbucks for a while but want to increase your earning potential.

Perk TV

https://www.reddit.com/r/perktv/

Like the subreddit devoted to Swagbucks, this subreddit focuses solely on Perk TV. If you're new to Perk TV, this subreddit site has a simple beginner tutorial that will teach you all the basics and a fantastic list of FAQs that will almost certainly answer any questions you might have. Because earning on Perk TV can be maximized by owning multiple devices, separate threads are all about cheap devices and buying/selling devices. If your questions aren't answered on any of the curated threads, the usual forum of user stories and questions has an active community of members, quick to comment and respond.

Warrior Forum

https://www.warriorforum.com/

The Warrior Forum is a large and active forum devoted to Internet marketing. Dozens of topics are covered, from copywriting to SEO to social media. Many of the topics discussed in this forum take plenty upfront work but can lead to huge passive income payoffs down the line. Some major players in the Internet marketing space are active on this forum, so it's a good place to virtually rub shoulders with people who have made Internet marketing work for them. If you're looking to learn a lot about passive income and don't mind putting in some time to sort through the mountains of information (some relevant and some not), this is a great site to bookmark and check often. With a large amount of active members, this forum is constantly updated with great information.

ADZbuzz

http://adzbuzzforum.com/forum/adzbuzz-passive-income-club-discussion

ADZbuzz is a community of like-minded people who are interested in creating passive income streams that make them more prosperous and financially secure. It is chock-full of great information for new and experienced passive income seekers.

Passive Income Streams

About the Author

Kristi Patrice Carter is a wife, mother, and serial entrepreneur who loves passive income. Kristi's lifelong goal is to positively impact people's lives, one self-help book at a time. With a BA in English from the University of Illinois at Chicago, a Juris Doctorate from Chicago Kent College of Law, and over 17 years of writing and marketing experience, Kristi has penned books about making money, living and thriving with chronic health issues, parenting, relationships, marketing, writing, and more.

Kristi has a passion for sharing her knowledge and hopes to inspire and empower readers around the world.

www.ingramcontent.com/pod-product-compliance
Lightning Source LLC
Chambersburg PA
CBHW060348190526
45169CB00002B/517